CELEBRATE
THE
THIRD
MILLENNIUM

CELEBRATE
THE
THIRD
MILLENNIUM

Facing the Future

with Hope

POPE JOHN PAUL II

Selected and arranged with an introduction by
PAUL THIGPEN

SERVANT PUBLICATIONS
ANN ARBOR, MICHIGAN

Charis Books is an imprint of Servant Publications especially designed to serve
Roman Catholics.

Published by Servant Publications
P.O. Box 8617
Ann Arbor, Michigan 48107

Cover design: Paul Higdon
Cover photograph: CORBIS/Owen Franken. Used by permission

99 00 01 02 03 10 9 8 7 6 5 4 3

Printed in the United States of America
ISBN 1-56955-120-0

Cataloging-in-Publication Data on file at the Library of Congress.

CONTENTS

THE JUBILEE:

A Call to Celebrate,
a Call to a Way of Life

The inscription on the famed Liberty Bell is recognized by millions of Americans: "Proclaim liberty throughout the land!" Perhaps fewer, though, know that these words come not from Benjamin Franklin, Thomas Jefferson, or some other of our nation's founders, but rather from the Bible. With this command, God instructed the ancient Hebrews to celebrate a festival—the Jubilee (see Lv 25:10).

The ram's horn trumpet blasted the announcement every fiftieth year, when the people were called to a special season of repentance, reconciliation, remission, and rejoicing. The Hebrew word in the proclamation that we translate "liberty" could also be rendered "freedom," "release," or "pardon." In this year, separated family members were to return home. Alienated property was to revert to its original owners. The land was to enjoy a rest. Hebrew slaves were to be set free. Debts were to be canceled. "For it is a Jubilee," God said; "it shall be holy to you" (Lv 25:12, RSV).

Familiar with this ancient tradition, medieval Christians associated the number fifty with the idea of remission, and the first Christian Jubilee was instituted by Pope Boniface VIII in the year 1300. A number of such celebrations have been held since then. But throughout history the Jubilee themes have remained constant: repentance, reconciliation, remission, rejoicing. Each of these Holy Years has invited a new generation of Christians to do penance; to mend broken relationships with God and with others; to have sins forgiven and spiritual debts canceled; and to join millions of fellow believers in praising God for the resulting new liberty in their lives.

In honor of the two-thousandth anniversary (by common reckoning) of our Lord's birth, Pope John Paul II has declared a Great Jubilee for the millennial year. He has called all Christians to a series of spiritual preparations as well in the three years leading up to the event. As a Holy Year, he has noted, the turn of the millennium is "a time when Jesus' invitation to conversion makes itself more deeply felt."[1] Through many ancient spiritual remedies—prayer, penance, reception of the Sacraments, pilgrimage, indulgence, sacrificial acts of charity and justice—Catholics in particular have precious opportunities to draw close to God by making use of the spiritual treasures of the Church.

Yet John Paul has made it clear throughout his pontificate that the Jubilee year actually clarifies and intensifies a call that has always issued from heaven to earth, a perennial vocation to holiness that requires our continual response. Jubilee, after all, isn't simply a season. It is a way of life.

In response to the Jubilee call, the U.S. Catholic Bishops' Subcommittee on the Third Millennium has offered a number

---

1. *Incarnationis Mysterium,* the Bull of Indictment for the Jubilee Year 2000, November 29, 1998.

of ideas for fleshing out the Holy Year celebration, including suggestions for both parishes and individuals. The subcommittee has recommended specifically "nine ways to live Jubilee and be a holy person." Individual Catholics can take these suggestions to heart by making practical changes in their lives reflecting the priorities of the Holy Year proclamation.[2]

These nine personal strategies form the framework for the present volume of readings from the work of the Holy Father. Clearly, John Paul has spent many years attempting to "live the Jubilee" both publicly and privately. His reflections on what it means to do so can thus provide us with wisdom and inspiration for our own attempts to live a holy life.

To live aright, we must first see aright. From his historical vantage point as the successor of Saint Peter, and his global vantage point as Universal Bishop, the pope is able to scan the horizons of history and culture, politics and society, to survey the conditions of our time. More importantly, the profound spiritual depth of this holy man has given the eyes of his soul a gift of penetrating discernment that goes beyond the conditions of our time to perceive the signs of the times. The first chapter of this book, then, brings together a number of observations John Paul has made about our moment in history, our present world's unique constellation of opportunities and crises, strengths and weaknesses, gifts and debts. In short, he

---

2. See the subcommittee's publication *Open Wide the Doors to Christ: A Framework to Implement "Tertio Millennio Adveniente"* (Washington, D.C.: The United States Catholic Conference, 1997), especially appendix C, "Some Personal Strategies to Prepare for the Jubilee Year"; these appear as well, slightly modified, in the brochure "Preparing for the Jubilee Year 2000: A Parishioner's Guide," also published by the USCC.

reads for us the signs of danger and the signs of hope in a world that desperately needs the witness of men and women living the Jubilee.

With this perspective as a context for the contemporary call to holiness, the book continues with a chapter of readings related to each of the nine personal strategies:

1. *Make time for prayer.*
2. *Practice forgiveness.*
3. *Celebrate the Eucharist.*
4. *Live a just life.*
5. *Help the poor.*
6. *Be a domestic church.*
7. *Share faith.*
8. *Join a small Christian community.*
9. *Know your faith.*

Here, then, is a strategy for personal holiness guaranteed to challenge and revolutionize us as individuals if we take it to heart. And what of the world as a whole? Can we hope to see it revolutionized as well?

God alone knows what the immediate future holds for a world that seems so perversely intent on destroying itself. Armed conflicts erupting across the globe ... nuclear weapons still pointed at massive population centers ... corrupt government officials leaving a wake of cynicism and despair ... the widening gap between rich and poor ... the rape of the environment ... the limits and fragility of even our most sophisticated technology. Our civilization's moral fiber lies in shreds; the proclamation of the Christian truth is undermined by false teachers within the Church even as it is assaulted by enemies without. All these warning signs of the gathering darkness, John Paul has pointed out to us.

And yet, he calls us nevertheless to hope. "The light shines in the darkness, and the darkness has not overcome it" (Jn 1:5, RSV). The Holy Father sees a morning star in the distance, insists that the winter must give way in the new millennium to "a springtime for the gospel." The spiritual hunger of our time is itself a good sign.

Of course, the gospel can bud and blossom in the worst of conditions. Adversity drives us to our knees, which is the best posture, after all, for prayer. That may even explain why John Paul has exhorted his listeners repeatedly to be prepared for martyrdom. The blood of the martyrs is still the seed of the Church.

Whichever way the world may go, it will go as it is driven by Providence and by the free choices of the human creatures who daily shape its course. No wonder, then, that human liberty remains one of John Paul's most insistent themes. The divine gift of free will is part of the divine image in us. When we choose against God, against truth, against life, we squander the gift, we erode the image, we lose the freedom.

All the more reason to celebrate the Third Millennium. All the more reason for the Holy Father—and for each of us, by a holy life—to "proclaim liberty throughout the land."

Paul Thigpen

SIGNS OF THE TIMES

You know how to interpret the appearance of earth and sky;
but why do you not know how to interpret the present time?

LUKE 12:56 RSV

Seeing history with the eyes of faith ... Jesus, the center
of history ... contradictions of the modern world ...
understanding the times ... the sign of the martyrs ...
the witness of ecumenism ... specific challenges to action
in the world today ... listen to the Holy Spirit

The world and the events of history cannot be understood in depth without professing faith in the God who is at work in them. Faith sharpens the inner eye, opening the mind to discover in the flux of events the workings of Providence. [FR 16]

Jesus is the genuine newness which surpasses all human expectations, and such He remains for ever, from age to age. The Incarnation of the Son of God and the salvation which He has accomplished by His death and resurrection are therefore the true criterion for evaluating all that happens in time and every effort to make life more human. [IM]

Faith teaches us that man's destiny is written in the heart and mind of God, who directs the course of history. It also teaches us that the Father puts in our hands the task of beginning to build here on earth the kingdom of heaven which the Son came to announce and which will find its fulfillment at the end of time.

It is our duty, then, to live in history, side by side with our peers, sharing their worries and hopes, because the Christian is and must be fully a man of his time. He cannot escape into another dimension, ignoring the tragedies of his era, closing his eyes and heart to the anguish that pervades life. On the contrary, it is he who, though not *of* this world, is immersed *in* this world every day, ready to hasten to wherever there is a brother in need of help, a tear to be dried, a request for help to be answered. On this we will be judged! [YP]

The modern world, despite its many successes, continues to be marked by contradictions. Progress in industry and agriculture has brought a higher standard of living to millions of people and offers great hope for many others. Technology has shrunk distances, while information has become instantaneous and has made possible new advances in human knowledge. Respect for the environment is growing and becoming a way of life. A great army of volunteers, whose generosity often remains hidden, is working tirelessly in every part of the world for the good of humanity, sparing no effort especially in meeting the needs of the poor and the suffering.

How can we fail to acknowledge with joy these positive aspects of our times? Unfortunately, however, the present world scene also presents more than a few negative signs. These include materialism and a growing contempt for human life, which have now assumed disturbing proportions. Many people live their lives with no other allegiance than to the laws of profit, prestige, and power. [WD]

In the East the atheistic regimes have left spiritual deserts in the hearts of many people, especially those of the young, while in the West there is the danger of an excessive concern with consumerism, which threatens to suffocate the spiritual values of society. The new evangelization is therefore the order of the day. [EL]

One of the phenomena which can be considered typical of modern culture [is] drug taking and addiction. Drugs are, in fact, … a symptom of a deeper weakness and illness, which especially affects the younger generations who are more exposed to a culture that is poor in genuine values. At a time like ours, in which man is able to bend even the laws of nature to his will, drug addiction with its capacity for damaging the person's willpower is an obstacle that reveals the intimate fragility of the human being and his need for help from the world that surrounds him, and—even more radically—from Him who alone can act in the depth of his psyche in difficulty. The relationship with God, lived in an attitude of authentic faith, is an extraordinarily effective support on the journey to recovery from humanly desperate situations. [TC]

The proportion of media programs which deal with religious and spiritual aspirations, programs which are morally uplifting and help people to live better lives, is apparently decreasing. It is not easy to remain optimistic about the positive influence of the mass media when they appear either to ignore the vital role of religion in the people's lives, or when the treatment that religious belief receives seems consistently negative and unsympathetic. Some elements of the media—especially in the entertainment sectors—often seem to wish to portray religious believers in the worst possible light.

Is there still a place for Christ in the traditional mass media? May we claim a place for Him in the new media? [WC]

While acknowledging the right to due freedom of information, one cannot acquiesce in treating moral evil as an occasion for sensationalism. Public opinion often feeds on sensationalism and the mass media play a particular role therein. In fact, the search for sensationalism leads to the loss of something which is essential to the morality of society. Harm is done to the fundamental right of individuals not to be easily exposed to the ridicule of public opinion. Even more, a distorted view of human life is created....

There is already sufficient proof that the prevalence of violence and impropriety in the mass media has become a source of scandal. Evil can indeed be sensational, but the sensationalism surrounding it is always dangerous for morality.

Therefore, the words of Christ about scandal apply also to all those persons and institutions, often anonymous, that through sensationalism in various ways open the door to evil in the conscience and behavior of vast segments of society, especially among the young, who are particularly vulnerable. "Woe to the world because of scandals!" (see Mt 18:7). Woe to societies where scandal becomes an everyday event. [LB]

Throughout the world legislation has been approved which contains elements in opposition to man's basic needs and values. I am thinking in particular of the legalization of abortion and euthanasia.... These laws are unjust, harmful to the good of man and society, and such as to alter the very concepts of law and democracy.

The near future is likely to bring new legislative enactments regarding man's intervention in his own life, his bodily nature and the environment. We are witnessing the birth of bio-rights and bio-politics. It is all the more important that we are committed to ensuring that this process takes place with respect for man's nature, whose demands are expressed by the natural law. [PL]

The conquest and exploitation of resources has become predominant and invasive, and today it has even reached the point of threatening the environment's hospitable aspect: The environment as "resource" risks threatening the environment as "home." [EH]

S cience, separated from the authentic values that
define the person, can deteriorate to the level of an
experimental exercise to satisfy the law of supply
and demand. Instead of responding to man's deep needs,
it is then limited to producing partial solutions for his
immediate requirements. Thus the intimate connection
which links man's activity with the depths of his being,
created in God's image, is cut short.

The historical task that unites believers and men of
goodwill in scientific research consists in promoting,
beyond all juridical convention, whatever favors human
dignity. [GE]

Among [the separated] Churches tolerance alone is certainly not enough. What kind of brothers and sisters are people who only tolerate one another? We also need to accept one another.... But we cannot be content even with mutual acceptance. For the Lord of history is bringing us to the third millennium of Christianity. A great hour is striking. Our reply should be equal to the great moment of this special *kairos* of God....

Tolerance is not enough! Mutual acceptance is not enough! Jesus Christ, He who is and who is to come, expects from us a visible sign of unity, a joint witness.

Sisters and brothers, I come to you with this message. I ask for a joint witness borne to Christ before the world. I ask this in the name of Christ! [EP]

In order to ensure that the new millennium … will witness a new flourishing of the human spirit, mediated through an authentic culture of freedom, men and women must learn to conquer fear. We must learn not to be afraid, we must rediscover a spirit of hope and a spirit of trust. Hope is not an empty optimism springing from a naïve confidence that the future will necessarily be better than the past. Hope and trust are the premise of responsible activity and are nurtured in that inner sanctuary of conscience where man is alone with God and thus perceives that he is not alone amid the enigmas of existence—for he is surrounded by the love of the Creator! [UN]

This century now drawing to a close has known very many martyrs, especially because of Nazism, Communism, and racial or tribal conflicts. People from every sector of society have suffered for their faith, paying with their blood for their fidelity to Christ and the Church, or courageously facing interminable years of imprisonment and privations of every kind because they refused to yield to an ideology which had become a pitiless dictatorial regime. From the psychological point of view, martyrdom is the most eloquent proof of the truth of the faith, for faith can give a human face even to the most violent of deaths and show its beauty even in the midst of the most atrocious persecutions. [IM]

L ife is a talent entrusted to us so that we can transform it and increase it, making it a gift to others (see Mt 25:14-30). No man is an iceberg drifting on the ocean of history. Each one of us belongs to a great family, in which he has his own place and his own role to play. Selfishness makes people deaf and dumb; love opens eyes and hearts, enabling people to make that original and irreplaceable contribution which—together with the thousands of deeds of so many brothers and sisters, often distant and unknown—converges to form the mosaic of charity which can change the tide of history. [YP]

The problems facing us are immense, but future generations will ask us to account for the way in which we have exercised our responsibilities. More than that, we are accountable to the Lord of history. [SS]

It is the Spirit of Christ who is at work in the Church and in history: We must listen to Him in order to recognize the signs of the new times and to make the expectation of the glorified Lord's return ever more vibrant in the hearts of the faithful. [IM]

NINE WAYS TO LIVE JUBILEE AND BE A HOLY PERSON

Proclaim liberty throughout the land to all its inhabitants; it shall be a jubilee for you…. It shall be holy to you…. You shall not wrong one another, but you shall fear your God; for I am the Lord your God. Therefore you shall do my statutes, and keep my ordinances and perform them; so you will dwell in the land securely.

LEVITICUS 25:10, 12, 17-18, RSV

Make time for prayer … practice forgiveness … celebrate the Eucharist … live a just life … help the poor … be a domestic church … share faith … join a small Christian community … know your faith

1
MAKE TIME
FOR PRAYER

Rejoice always, pray constantly, give thanks in all circumstances; for
this is the will of God in Christ Jesus for you.

1 THESSALONIANS 5:17-18, RSV

Prayer, as essential as breathing ... the center of our lives ...
intimacy with God ... a contemplative outlook ... action and
contemplation ... turning to the Source ... learning the Father
... the Holy Spirit and prayer ... pilgrimage ... the bond of
prayer ... prayer with the saints

Prayer particularly belongs to the Christian religion, in which it occupies a central position. Jesus urges us to "pray always without becoming weary" (Lk 18:1, NAB). Christians know that for them prayer is as essential as breathing, and once they have tasted the sweetness of intimate conversation with God, they do not hesitate to immerse themselves in it with trusting abandonment. [CP]

In our bodies we are a mere speck in the vast created universe, but by virtue of our souls we transcend the whole material world. [NY]

Prayer makes us aware that everything—even evil—finds its principal and definitive reference point in God. [LB]

Prayer is not one occupation among many, but is at the center of our life in Christ. It turns our attention away from ourselves and directs it to the Lord. Prayer fills the mind with truth and gives hope to the heart. Without a deep experience of prayer, growth in the moral life will be shallow. [NE]

"Lord, teach us to pray" (Lk 11:1, RSV). When, on the slopes of the Mount of Olives, the apostles addressed Jesus with these words, they were not asking an ordinary question, but with spontaneous trust, they were expressing one of the deepest needs of the human heart.

To tell the truth, today's world does not make much room for that need. The hectic pace of daily activity, combined with the noisy and often frivolous invasiveness of the means of communication, is certainly not something conducive to the interior recollection required for prayer. Then, too, there are deeper difficulties: modern people have an increasingly less religious view of the world and life. The secularization process seems to have persuaded them that the course of events can be sufficiently explained by the interplay of this world's immanent forces, independent of higher intervention. The achievements of science and technology have also fostered their conviction that they already have, and will continue to increase, their ability to dominate situations, directing them according to their own desires.

[Nevertheless,] because they are creatures and of themselves incomplete and needy, human beings spontaneously turn to Him who is the Source of every gift, in order to praise Him, make intercession, and in Him seek to fulfill the tormenting desire which enflames their hearts. [CP]

We need ... to foster, in ourselves and in others, a contemplative outlook. Such an outlook arises from faith in the God of life, who has created every individual as a wonder (see Ps 139:14). It is the outlook of those who see life in its deeper meaning, who grasp its utter gratuitousness, its beauty and its invitation to freedom and responsibility. It is the outlook of those who do not presume to take possession of reality but instead accept it as a gift, discovering in all things the reflection of the Creator and seeing in every person His living image (see Gn 1:27; Ps 8:5).

This outlook does not give into discouragement when confronted by those who are sick, suffering, outcast, or at death's door. Instead, in all these situations it feels challenged to find meaning, and precisely in the face of every person [it finds] a call to encounter, dialogue, and solidarity.

It is time for all of us to adopt this outlook, and with deep religious awe to rediscover the ability to revere and honor every person.... Inspired by this contemplative outlook, the new people of the redeemed cannot but respond with songs of joy, praise, and thanksgiving for the priceless gift of life, for the mystery of every individual's call to share through Christ in the life of grace and in an existence of unending communion with God our Creator and Father. [EV]

To take time to pray, and to nourish prayer and activities through biblical, theological, and doctrinal study; to live by Christ and His grace by receiving assiduously the sacraments of reconciliation and the Eucharist—such are the fundamental requirements of every deeply Christian life. Thus the Holy Spirit will be the source both of your action and of your contemplation, which will then interpenetrate each other, support each other, and yield abundant fruit.

This deep unity between prayer and action is at the basis of all spiritual renewal, especially among the laity. It is at the basis of the great enterprises of evangelization and construction of the world according to God's plan. [PA]

The breath of the divine life, the Holy Spirit, in its simplest and most common manner, expresses itself and makes itself felt in prayer.... Wherever people are praying in the world, there the Holy Spirit is, the living breath of prayer. [DV 65]

Prayer always remains the voice of all those who apparently have no voice. [DV 65]

P rayer is ... the revelation of that abyss which is the heart of man: a depth which comes from God and which only God can fill, precisely with the Holy Spirit. [DV 65]

The Holy Spirit not only enables us to pray, but guides us from within in prayer: He is present in our prayer and gives it a divine dimension.... Prayer through the power of the Holy Spirit becomes the ever more mature expression of the new man, who by means of this prayer participates in the divine life. [DV 65]

"Our Father who art in heaven ..." (Mt 6:9, RSV).

According to [these words]—Christ's answer to the request "teach us to pray"—everything is reduced to this single concept: to learn to pray means "to learn the Father." If we learn the Father in the full sense of the word, in its full dimension, we have learned everything. [LP]

To learn who the Father is means learning what absolute trust is. To learn the Father means acquiring the certainty that ... He does not refuse you even when everything—materially and psychologically—seems to indicate refusal. He never refuses you. [LP]

The mission of reconciliation is proper to the whole Church, also and especially to that Church which has already been admitted to the full sharing in divine glory with the Virgin Mary—the angels and the saints, who contemplate and adore the thrice-holy God. The Church in heaven, the Church on earth, and the Church in purgatory are mysteriously united in this cooperation with Christ in reconciling the world to God.

The first means of this [saving] action is that of prayer. It is certain that the Blessed Virgin, mother of Christ and of the Church, and the saints, who have now reached the end of their earthly journey and possess God's glory, sustain by their intercession their brethren who are on pilgrimage through the world, in the commitment to conversion, to faith, to getting up again after every fall, to acting in order to help the growth of communion and peace in the Church and in the world. In the mystery of the communion of saints, universal reconciliation is accomplished in its most profound form, which is also the most fruitful for the salvation of all. [RP]

I wish to reaffirm the need for intense, humble, confident, and persevering prayer, if the world is finally to become a dwelling place of peace. Prayer is *par excellence* the power needed to implore that peace and obtain it. It gives courage and support to all who love this good and desire to promote it in accordance with their own possibilities and in the various situations in which they live.

Prayer not only opens us up to a meeting with the Most High but also disposes us to a meeting with our neighbor, helping us to establish with everyone, without discrimination, relationships of respect, understanding, esteem, and love.... Prayer, as the authentic expression of a right relationship with God and with others, is already a positive contribution to peace. [WP]

rayer is the bond which most effectively unites us. It is through prayer that believers meet one another at a level where inequalities, misunderstandings, bitterness, and hostility are overcome, namely before God, the Lord and Father of all. [WP]

If the shrines of the world are the image of the heavenly Jerusalem, pilgrimage is the image of our human life…. Pilgrimage is a fundamental and foundational experience of the believer's condition as *homo viator*, a person on the road to the Source of all good and toward fulfillment. In putting all of his being on the move, his body, his heart, and his intelligence, man discovers himself to be a seeker of God and pilgrim of the eternal. He tears himself away from himself to pass over to God. He is freed from false certitudes, returns to his natural condition of Prodigal Son called to forgiveness by the tenderness of the Father who awaits him. These simple things are better learned through experience than from books! [PS]

America needs much prayer—
lest it lose its soul. [LB]

All human life, and therefore all human time, must become praise of the Creator and thanksgiving to him. But man's relationship with God also *demands times of explicit prayer*, in which the relationship becomes an intense dialogue, involving every dimension of the person. "The Lord's Day" is the day of this relationship *par excellence* when men and women raise their song to God and become the voice of all creation.

This is precisely why it is also *the day of rest*. Speaking vividly as it does of renewal and detachment, the interruption of the often-oppressive rhythm of work expresses the dependence of man and the cosmos upon God. *Everything belongs to God!* The Lord's Day returns again and again to declare this principle within the weekly reckoning of time. The "Sabbath" has therefore been interpreted evocatively as a determining element in the kind of "sacred architecture" of time which marks biblical revelation. It recalls that *the universe and history belong to God*; and without a constant awareness of that truth, man cannot serve in the world as coworker of the Creator. [DD]

2
PRACTICE
FORGIVENESS

Put on, then, as God's chosen ones, holy and beloved, compassion, kindness, lowliness, meekness, and patience, forbearing one another and, if one has a complaint against another, forgiving each other; as the Lord has forgiven you, so you also must forgive.

COLOSSIANS 3:12-13, RSV

The sacrament of penance ... the nature of sin and repentance ... the Church, mediatrix of reconciliation ... living the truth ... a merciful Father ... indulgences ... false morality ... examination of conscience ... forgiving others ... the logic of love ... the healing of memories ... the freedom of forgiveness ... forgiveness and justice

The sacrament of penance offers the sinner a new possibility to convert and to recover the grace of justification won by the sacrifice of Christ. The sinner thus enters the life of God anew and shares fully in the life of the Church. Confessing his own sins, the believer truly receives pardon and can once more take part in the Eucharist as the sign that he has again found communion with the Father and with His Church.

From the first centuries, however, the Church has always been profoundly convinced that pardon, freely granted by God, implies in consequence a real change of life, the gradual elimination of evil within, a renewal in our way of living. The sacramental action had to be combined with an existential act, with a real cleansing from fault, precisely what is called penance. Pardon does not imply that this existential process becomes superfluous, but rather that it acquires a meaning, that it is accepted and welcomed. [IM]

In the sacrament of penance, the sacrament of confession and reconciliation, every soul relives as its personal history the Gospel account of the tax collector, who left the temple justified: "But the tax collector, standing far off, would not even lift up his eyes to heaven, but beat his breast, saying, 'God, be merciful to me a sinner!' I tell you, this man went down to his house justified rather than the other; for every one who exalts himself will be humbled, but he who humbles himself will be exalted" (Lk 18:13-14, RSV).

To acknowledge one's misery in the sight of God is not to abase oneself, but to live the truth of one's own condition and thus to obtain the true greatness of justice and grace after falling into sin, the effect of malice and weakness. It is to rise to the loftiest peace of spirit, by rising into a living relationship with God who is merciful and faithful. The truth thus lived is the only thing in the human condition that makes us free. [AP]

Sin's essential nature is that of an offense against God. This is an important fact which includes the perverse act of the creature who knowingly and freely opposes the will of his Creator and Lord, violating the law of good and freely submitting to the yoke of evil. It is an offense against the divine Majesty.... We must say that it is also an act which offends the divine charity in that it is an infraction of the law of friendship and covenant which God has established for His people and every person in the blood of Christ. Therefore it is an act of infidelity, and, in practice, a rejection of His love.

Sin, therefore, is not a simple human error, nor does it cause damage only to the person. It is an offense against God in that the sinner disobeys the law of the Creator and Lord, and thus offends His paternal love. Sin draws its significance from the person's relationship to God.

It is Jesus who, especially in the parable of the Prodigal Son, makes us understand that sin is an offense against the love of the Father in His description of the son's outrageous scorn for his father's authority and house.... The great gift which Jesus gives us in this parable is the comforting and reassuring revelation of the merciful love of a Father who, with his arms open wide, awaits the Prodigal Son's return, hurrying to embrace and pardon him, canceling all the consequences of sin and celebrating the feast of new life for him. [SP]

Sin is ... a wound inflicted upon the Church. In fact, every sin harms the holiness of the ecclesial community. Since all the faithful are in solidarity in the Christian community, there can never be a sin which does not have an effect on the whole community.... Reconciliation with God is also reconciliation with the Church, and in a certain sense with all of creation, whose harmony is violated by sin. The Church is the mediatrix of this reconciliation. It is a role assigned to her by her Founder, who gave her the mission and power of forgiving sins. Every instance of reconciliation with God thus takes place in an explicit or implicit, conscious or unconscious, relationship with the Church....

Without a doubt the power to pardon belongs to God, and the forgiveness of sins is the work of the Holy Spirit. Nevertheless, forgiveness comes from the application to the sinner of the redemption gained through the cross of Christ, who entrusted the Church with the mission and ministry of bringing salvation to the whole world in His name. Forgiveness, then, is asked of God and granted by God, but not independently of the Church founded by Jesus Christ for the salvation of all. [SP]

We know that in order to communicate the fruits of His passion and death to people, the risen Christ conferred on the apostles the power to forgive sins: "Whose sins you forgive are forgiven them, and whose sins you retain are retained" (Jn 20:23, NAB). In the Church the priests, as heirs of the mission and power of the apostles, forgive sins in Christ's name. However, we can say that in the sacrament of reconciliation the priest's specific ministry does not exclude, but rather includes, the exercise of the common priesthood of the faithful who confess their sins and ask for pardon under the influence of the Holy Spirit, who converts them intimately through the grace of Christ the Redeemer. [SP]

The Christian is never left alone, not even in the state of sin. He is always part of the priestly community which supports him with the solidarity of charity, fraternity, and prayer to obtain for him the grace of being restored to God's friendship and the company of the saints. The Church, the community of saints, in the sacrament of penance shows that she is a priestly community of mercy and forgiveness. [SP]

The truth [about ourselves], which comes from the Word and must lead us to Him, explains why sacramental confession must not stem from and be accompanied by a mere psychological impulse, as though the sacrament were a substitute for psychotherapy, but from sorrow based on supernatural motives—because sin violates charity towards God, the Supreme Good, [which] was the reason for the Redeemer's sufferings and causes us to lose the goods of eternity. [AP]

It is ... self-evident that [in sacramental confession] the accusation of sins must include the serious intention not to commit them again in the future. If this disposition of soul is lacking, then there is really no repentance. [AP]

Why do the consciences of young people not rebel ... against the moral evil which flows from personal choices? Why do so many acquiesce in attitudes and behavior which offend human dignity and disfigure the image of God in us? The normal thing would be for conscience to point out the mortal danger to the individual and to humanity contained in the easy acceptance of evil and sin. Is it because conscience itself is losing the ability to distinguish good from evil?

In a technological culture in which people are used to dominating matter, discovering its laws and mechanisms in order to transform it according to their wishes, the danger arises of also wanting to manipulate conscience and its demands. In a culture which holds that no universally valid truths are possible, nothing is absolute. Therefore, in the end—they say—objective goodness and evil no longer really matter. Good comes to mean what is pleasing or useful at a particular moment. Evil means what contradicts our subjective wishes. Each person can build a private system of values.

Young people, do not give in to this widespread false morality. Do not stifle your conscience! [YD]

Conscience is the most secret core and sanctuary of a person, where we are alone with God. "In the depths of his conscience man detects a law which he does not impose upon himself, but which holds him to obedience" (*Gaudium et spes*, n. 16). That law is not an external human law, but the voice of God, calling us to free ourselves from the grip of evil desires and sin, and stimulating us to seek what is good and true.

Only by listening to the voice of God in your most intimate being, and by acting in accordance with its directions, will you reach the freedom you yearn for. As Jesus said, only the truth will make you free (see Jn 8:32). And the truth is not the fruit of each individual's imagination. God gave you intelligence to know the truth, and your will to achieve what is morally good. He has given you the light of conscience to guide your moral decisions, to love good and avoid evil. [YD]

Moral truth is objective, and a properly formed conscience can perceive it. But if conscience itself has been corrupted, how can it be restored? If conscience—which is light—no longer enlightens, how can we overcome the moral darkness?

Jesus says: "The eye is the body's lamp. If your eyes are good, your body will be filled with light; if your eyes are bad, your body will be in darkness. And if your light is darkness, how deep will the darkness be!" (Mt 6:22-23, NAB). But Jesus also says: "I am the light of the world. No follower of Mine shall ever walk in darkness; no, he shall possess the light of life" (Jn 8:12, NAB).

If you follow Christ you will restore conscience to its rightful place and proper role, and you will be the light of the world, the salt of the earth (see Mt 5:13). A rebirth of conscience must come from two sources: first, the effort to know objective truth with certainty, including the truth about God; and secondly, the light of faith in Jesus Christ, who alone has the words of life. [YD]

Examination of conscience is ... one of the most decisive moments of life. It places each individual before the truth of his own life. Thus he discovers the distance which separates his deeds from the ideal which he had set himself. [IM]

Everything comes from Christ, but since we belong to Him, whatever is ours also becomes His and acquires a healing power. This is what is meant by "the treasures of the Church," which are the good works of the saints. To pray in order to gain [an] indulgence means to enter into this spiritual communion and therefore to open oneself totally to others.

In the spiritual realm, too, no one lives for himself alone. And salutary concern for the salvation of one's own soul is freed from fear and selfishness only when it becomes concern for the salvation of others as well. This is the reality of the communion of saints, the mystery of "vicarious life," of prayer as the means of union with Christ and His saints. He takes us with Him in order that we may weave with Him the white robe of the new humanity, the robe of bright linen which clothes the Bride of Christ. [IM]

Throughout His life Jesus proclaimed God's for-giveness, but He also taught the need for mutual forgiveness as the condition for obtaining it. In the Lord's Prayer He makes us pray: "Forgive us our trespasses, as we forgive those who trespass against us" (Mt 6:12, NAB). With that "as," He places in our hands the measure with which we shall be judged by God. The parable of the unforgiving servant, punished for his hardness of heart towards his fellow servant (see Mt 18:23-35), teaches us that those who are unwilling to forgive exclude themselves by this very fact from divine forgiveness: "So also my heavenly Father will do to every one of you, if you do not forgive your brother from your heart" (Mt 18:35, RSV).

Our prayer itself cannot be pleasing to the Lord unless it is preceded, and in a certain sense "guaranteed" in its authenticity, by a sincere effort on our part to be reconciled with our brother who has "something against us": Only then will it be possible for us to present an offering pleasing to God (see Mt 5:23-24). [WD]

As the Successor of Peter, I ask that ... the Church, strong in the holiness which she receives from her Lord, should kneel before God and implore forgiveness for the past and present sins of her sons and daughters. All have sinned and none can claim righteousness before God (see 1 Kgs 8:46). Let it be said once more without fear: "We have sinned" (Jer 3:25, RSV), but let us keep alive the certainty that "where sin increased, grace abounded all the more" (Rom 5:20, RSV). [IM]

With deep conviction I wish to appeal to everyone to seek peace along the paths of forgiveness. I am fully aware that forgiveness can seem contrary to human logic, which often yields to the dynamics of conflict and revenge. But forgiveness is inspired by the logic of love, that love which God has for every man and woman, for every people and nation, and for the whole human family.

If the Church dares to proclaim what, from a human standpoint, might appear to be sheer folly, it is precisely because of her unshakable confidence in the infinite love of God. As Scripture bears witness, God is rich in mercy and full of forgiveness for those who come back to Him…. God's forgiveness becomes in our hearts an inexhaustible source of forgiveness in our relationships with one another, helping us to live together in true brotherhood. [WD]

The difficulty of forgiving does not only arise from circumstances of the present. History carries with it a heavy burden of violence and conflict which cannot easily be shed. Abuses of power, oppression, and wars have brought suffering to countless human beings and, even if the causes of these sad events are lost in the distant past, their destructive effects live on, fueling fear, suspicion, hatred, and division among families, ethnic groups, and whole peoples. These are facts which sorely try the goodwill of those who are seeking to overcome their past conditioning.

The truth is that one cannot remain a prisoner of the past, for individuals and peoples need a sort of "healing of memories," so that past evils will not come back again. This does not mean forgetting past events; it means re-examining them with a new attitude and learning precisely from the experience of suffering that only love can build up, whereas hatred produces devastation and ruin. The deadly cycle of revenge must be replaced with the new-found liberty of forgiveness. [WD]

L asting peace ... is not just a matter of structures and mechanisms. It rests above all on the adoption of a style of human coexistence marked by mutual acceptance and a capacity to forgive from the heart. We all need to be forgiven by others, so we must all be ready to forgive. Asking and granting forgiveness is something profoundly worthy of man; sometimes it is the only way out of situations marked by age-old and violent hatred.

Certainly, forgiveness does not come spontaneously or naturally to people. Forgiving from the heart can sometimes be actually heroic. The pain of losing a child, a brother or sister, one's parents or whole family as a result of war, terrorism, or criminal acts can lead to the total closing of oneself to others. People who have been left with nothing because they have been deprived of their land and home, refugees and those who have endured the humiliation of violence, cannot fail to feel the temptation to hatred and revenge. Only the warmth of human relationships marked by respect, understanding, and acceptance can help them to overcome such feelings. The liberating encounter with forgiveness, though fraught with difficulties, can be experienced even by the wounded heart, thanks to the healing power of love, which has its first source in God who is Love. [WD]

Forgiveness, in its truest and highest form, is a free act of love. But precisely because it is an act of love, it has its own intrinsic demands: the first of which is respect for the truth.

God alone is absolute truth. But He made the human heart open to the desire for truth, which He then fully revealed in His Incarnate Son. Hence we are all called to live the truth. Where lies and falsehood are sown, there suspicion and division flourish.... Forgiveness, far from precluding the search for truth, actually requires it. The evil which has been done must be acknowledged and as far as possible corrected....

Another essential prerequisite for forgiveness and reconciliation is justice, which finds its ultimate foundation in the law of God and in His plan of love and mercy for humanity. Understood in this way, justice is not limited to establishing what is right between the parties in conflict but looks above all to re-establishing authentic relationships with God, with oneself, and with others. Thus there is no contradiction between forgiveness and justice. Forgiveness neither eliminates nor lessens the need for the reparation which justice requires, but seeks to reintegrate individuals and groups into society, and states into the community of nations. No punishment can suppress the inalienable dignity of those who have committed evil. The door to repentance and rehabilitation must always remain open. [WD]

C an we be fully reconciled with Christ without being fully reconciled among ourselves? Can we bear joint and effective witness to Christ if we are not reconciled with one another? Can we be reconciled with one another without forgiving one another? Forgiveness is the condition for reconciliation. But this cannot take place without interior transformation and conversion, which is the work of grace. [EP]

3
CELEBRATE
THE EUCHARIST

Jesus said to them: "Truly, truly, I say to you, unless you eat
the flesh of the Son of man and drink his blood, you have no
life in you; he who eats my flesh and drinks my blood has eter-
nal life, and I will raise him up at the last day. For my flesh is
food indeed and my blood is drink indeed. He who eats my
flesh and drinks my blood abides in me, and I in him."

JOHN 6:53-56, RSV

The source and summit of Christian life ... Jesus living
and real in our midst ... our sacrifices united with His ...
Sunday, the fundamental feast of the Church ... rediscov-
ering the Lord's Day ... the fountainhead of Church life ...
communion with the universal Church ... an "exercise of
desire" ... the Eucharist and witness ... the Eucharist and
charity, justice, and peace ... Sunday as "prophecy"

The Eucharist is the source of the Christian life because whoever shares in it receives the motivation and strength to live as a true Christian. Christ's sacrifice on the cross imparts to the believer the dynamism of His generous love; the Eucharistic banquet nourishes the faithful with the Body and Blood of the divine Lamb sacrificed for us, and it gives them the strength to follow in His footsteps.

The Eucharist is the summit of the whole Christian life because the faithful bring to it all their prayers and good works, their joys and sufferings. These modest offerings are united to the perfect sacrifice of Christ and are thus completely sanctified and lifted up to God in an act of perfect worship which brings the faithful into the divine intimacy. [HE]

For Christians, Sunday is "the fundamental feast day," established not only to mark the succession of time but to reveal time's deeper meaning. [DD]

For two thousand years, the Church has been the cradle in which Mary places Jesus and entrusts Him to the adoration and contemplation of all peoples. May the humility of the Bride cause to shine forth still more brightly the glory and power of the Eucharist, which she celebrates and treasures in her heart. In the sign of the consecrated Bread and Wine, Christ Jesus risen and glorified, the light of the nations (see Lk 2:32), reveals the enduring reality of His Incarnation. He remains living and real in our midst in order to nourish the faithful with His Body and Blood. [IM]

A parish's vocation can be defined only according to the Church's sacramental structure. It is here that Christ's presence in the paschal mystery is visibly signified. At Mass, the offerings of all converge: of happiness and suffering, apostolic efforts and fraternal services of all kinds. The Lord associates the sacrifices of His brothers and sisters with His own sacrifice. He gathers us in His Holy Spirit, He strengthens our faith and our charity, He listens to our petitions to the Father to extend reconciliation, salvation, and peace to the whole world, and unites us with the saints of every age as we wait for full communion in His kingdom. [AL]

The Lord's Day—as Sunday was called from apostolic times—has always been accorded special attention in the history of the Church because of its close connection with the very core of the Christian mystery. In fact, in the weekly reckoning of time Sunday recalls the day of Christ's resurrection. It is *Easter* which returns week by week, celebrating Christ's victory over sin and death, the fulfillment in Him of the first creation, and the dawn of "the new creation" (see 2 Cor 5:17). It is the day which recalls in grateful adoration the world's first day and looks forward in active hope to "the last day," when Christ will come in glory (see Acts 1:11; 1 Thes 4:13-17) and all things will be made new (see Rv 21:5). [DD]

The resurrection of Jesus is the fundamental event upon which Christian faith rests (see 1 Cor 15:14). It is an astonishing reality, fully grasped in the light of faith, yet historically attested to by those who were privileged to see the Risen Lord. It is a wondrous event which is not only absolutely unique in human history, but which lies *at the very heart of the mystery of time....* Therefore, in commemorating the day of Christ's resurrection not just once a year but every Sunday, the Church seeks to indicate to every generation the true fulcrum of history, to which the mystery of the world's origin and its final destiny leads. [DD]

The custom of the "weekend" has become more widespread, a weekly period of respite, spent perhaps far from home and often involving participation in cultural, political, or sporting activities which are usually held on free days. This social and cultural phenomenon is by no means without its positive aspects if, while respecting true values, it can contribute to people's development and to the advancement of the life of society as a whole. All of this responds not only to the need for rest, but also to the need for celebration which is inherent in our humanity.

Unfortunately, when Sunday loses its fundamental meaning and becomes merely part of a "weekend," it can happen that people stay locked within a horizon so limited that they can no longer see heaven. Hence, though ready to celebrate, they are really incapable of doing so. [DD]

I would strongly urge everyone to rediscover Sunday: *Do not be afraid to give your time to Christ!* Yes, let us open our time to Christ, that He may cast light upon it and give it direction. He is the One who knows the secret of time and the secret of eternity, and He gives us "His day" as an ever-new gift of His love.

The rediscovery of this day is a grace which we must implore, not only so that we may live the demands of faith to the full, but also so that we may respond concretely to the deepest human yearnings. Time given to Christ is never time lost, but is rather time gained, so that our relationships and indeed our whole life may become more profoundly human. [DD]

"I am with you always, to the end of the age" (Mt 28:20). This promise of Christ never ceases to resound in the Church as the fertile secret of her life and the wellspring of her hope. As the day of Resurrection, Sunday is not only the remembrance of a past event: It is a celebration of the living presence of the Risen Lord in the midst of His own people.

For this presence to be properly proclaimed and lived, it is not enough that the disciples of Christ pray individually and commemorate the death and resurrection of Christ inwardly, in the secrecy of their hearts. Those who have received the grace of baptism are not saved as individuals alone, but as members of the Mystical Body, having become part of the People of God. It is important therefore that they come together to express fully the very identity of the Church, the *ekklesia*, the assembly called together by the Risen Lord who offered His life to reunite "the scattered children of God" (Jn 11:52, NIV).

They have become "one" in Christ (see Gal 3:28) through the gift of the Spirit. This unity becomes visible when Christians gather together: It is then that they come to know vividly and to testify to the world that they are the people redeemed, drawn "from every tribe and language and people and nation" (Rv 5:9). [DD]

The Eucharist is not only a particularly intense expression of the reality of the Church's life, but also in a sense its fountainhead. The Eucharist feeds and forms the Church: "Because there is one bread, we who are many are one body, for we all partake of the one bread" (1 Cor 10:17, RSV). Because of this vital link with the sacrament of the Body and Blood of the Lord, the mystery of the Church is savored, proclaimed, and lived supremely in the Eucharist. [DD]

At Sunday Mass, Christians relive with particular intensity the experience of the apostles on the evening of Easter when the Risen Lord appeared to them as they were gathered together (see Jn 20:19). In a sense, the People of God of all times were present in that small nucleus of disciples, the first fruits of the Church. Through their testimony, every generation of believers hears the greeting of Christ, rich with the messianic gift of peace, won by His blood and offered with His Spirit: "Peace be with you!" [DD]

In celebrating the Eucharist, the community opens itself to communion with the universal Church, imploring the Father to "remember the Church throughout the world" and make her grow in the unity of all the faithful with the pope and with the pastors of the particular Churches, until love is brought to perfection. [DD]

Sunday after Sunday the Church moves toward the
final "Lord's Day," that Sunday which knows no
end. The expectation of Christ's coming is
inscribed in the very mystery of the Church and is evi-
denced in every Eucharistic celebration. But, with its specific remembrance of the glory of the Risen Christ, the
Lord's Day recalls with greater intensity the future glory
of His return.

This makes Sunday the day on which the Church,
showing forth more clearly her identity as "Bride,"
anticipates in some sense the eschatological reality of the
heavenly Jerusalem. Gathering her children into the
Eucharistic assembly and teaching them to wait for the
"divine Bridegroom," she engages in a kind of exercise of
desire, receiving a foretaste of the joy of the new heavens
and new earth, when the holy city, the new Jerusalem,
will come down from God, "prepared as a bride adorned
for her husband" (Rv 21:2, RSV). [DD]

The Mass ... *truly makes present the sacrifice of the Cross.* Under the species of bread and wine, upon which has been invoked the outpouring of the Spirit who works with absolutely unique power in the words of consecration, Christ offers Himself to the Father in the same act of sacrifice by which He offered Himself on the Cross. [DD]

Receiving the Bread of Life, the disciples of Christ ready themselves to undertake with the strength of the Risen Lord and his Spirit *the tasks which await them in their ordinary life*. For the faithful who have understood the meaning of what they have done, the Eucharistic celebration does not stop at the church door. Like the first witnesses of the resurrection, Christians who gather each Sunday to experience and proclaim the presence of the Risen Lord are called *to evangelize and bear witness* in their daily lives.... Once the assembly disperses, Christ's disciples return to their everyday surroundings with the commitment to make their whole life a gift, a spiritual sacrifice pleasing to God (see Rom 12:1). {DD}

Today, as in the heroic times of the beginning [of the Church], many who wish to live in accord with the demands of their faith are being faced with difficult situations in various parts of the world. They live in surroundings which are sometimes decidedly hostile and at other times—more frequently, in fact—indifferent and unresponsive to the gospel message. If believers are not to be overwhelmed, they must be able to count on the support of the Christian community. This is why they must be convinced that it is crucially important for the life of faith that they should come together with others on Sundays to celebrate the Passover of the Lord in the sacrament of the New Covenant. [DD]

The Christian community [has] the duty to make the Eucharist the place where fraternity becomes practical solidarity, where the last are the first in the minds and attentions of the brethren, where Christ Himself—through the generous gifts from the rich to the very poor—may somehow prolong in time the miracle of the multiplication of the loaves. [DD]

W hy not make the Lord's Day a more intense time of sharing, encouraging all the inventiveness of which Christian charity is capable? Inviting to a meal people who are alone, visiting the sick, providing food for needy families, spending a few hours in voluntary work and acts of solidarity: These would certainly be ways of bringing into people's lives the love of Christ received at the Eucharistic table.

Lived in this way, not only the Sunday Eucharist but the whole of Sunday becomes a great school of charity, justice, and peace. The presence of the Risen Lord in the midst of His people becomes an undertaking of solidarity, a compelling force for inner renewal, an inspiration to change the structures of sin in which individuals, communities, and at times entire peoples are entangled. Far from being an escape, the Christian Sunday is a "prophecy" inscribed on time itself, a prophecy obliging the faithful to follow in the footsteps of the One who came "to preach good news to the poor ... to proclaim release to the captives and recovering of sight to the blind, to set at liberty those who are oppressed, [and] to proclaim the acceptable year of the Lord" (Lk 4:18-19, RSV). In the Sunday commemoration of Easter, believers learn from Christ, and remembering His promise, "I leave you peace, my peace I give you" (see Jn 14:27), they become in their turn *builders of peace*. [DD]

Since Sunday is the weekly Easter, recalling and making present the day upon which Christ rose from the dead, it is also the day which reveals the meaning of time. It has nothing in common with the cosmic cycles according to which natural religion and human culture tend to impose a structure on time, succumbing perhaps to the myth of eternal return. The Christian Sunday is wholly other! Springing from the resurrection, it cuts through human time, the months, the years, the centuries, like a directional arrow which points them toward their target: Christ's Second Coming. Sunday foreshadows the last day, the day of the *Parousia*, which in a way is already anticipated by Christ's glory in the event of the resurrection.

In fact, everything that will happen until the end of the world will be no more than an extension and unfolding of what happened on the day when the battered body of the crucified Lord was raised by the power of the Spirit and became in turn the wellspring of the Spirit for all humanity. Christians know that there is no need to wait for another time of salvation, since, however long the world may last, they are already living in *the last times*.

Not only the Church, but the cosmos itself and

history are ceaselessly ruled and governed by the glorified Christ. It is this life-force which propels creation, "groaning in birth-pangs until now" (see Rom 8:22), toward the goal of its full redemption. Mankind can have only a faint intuition of this process, but Christians have the key and the certainty. Keeping Sunday holy is the important witness which they are called to bear, so that every stage of human history will be upheld by hope. [DD]

The Eucharist is the full realization of the worship which humanity owes to God, and it cannot be compared to any other religious experience.... The risen Lord ... calls the faithful together to give them the light of His Word and the nourishment of His Body as the perennial sacramental wellspring of redemption. The grace flowing from this wellspring renews mankind, life, and history. [DD]

As a day of prayer, communion, and joy, Sunday resounds throughout society, emanating vital energies and reasons for hope. Sunday is the proclamation that time, in which He who is the Risen Lord of history makes His home, is not the grave of our illusions but the cradle of an ever-new future, an opportunity given to us to turn the fleeting moments of this life into seeds of eternity. Sunday is an invitation to look ahead; it is the day on which the Christian community cries out to Christ, "*Maranatha*: O Lord, come!" (1 Cor 16:22, NAB). With this cry of hope and expectation, the Church is the companion and support of human hope. From Sunday to Sunday, enlightened by Christ, she goes forward towards the unending Sunday of the heavenly Jerusalem. [DD]

4
LIVE A JUST LIFE

*He has showed you, O man, what is good; and what does the
Lord require of you but to do justice, and to love kindness, and
to walk humbly with your God?*

MICAH 6:8, RSV

Love God and neighbor ... humanity as the image of God
... the nature of true freedom ... moral accountability ...
challenges to Americans ... respect for life ... the trivialization of sexuality ... the roles of women ... respecting
differences ... the culture of peace ... solidarity with
migrants ... nationalism versus patriotism ... the universal moral law ... labor worthy of human dignity ...
respect for God's creation

Charity is … the high road that will lead us to the goal of the Great Jubilee. To reach this appointment, we need to be able to confront ourselves and undertake a rigorous examination of conscience, the indispensable premise for a radical conversion, which can transform our life and give it an authentic meaning which enables believers to love God with all their heart, with all their soul, and with all their strength, and to love their neighbor as themselves (see Lk 10:27).

By conforming your daily life to the gospel of the one Teacher who has "the words of eternal life," you will be able to become genuine workers for justice, following the commandment which makes love the new frontier of Christian witness. This is the law for transforming the world. [YP]

Precisely because man is a person, his dignity is unique among all creatures. Every individual man is an end in himself and can never be used as a mere means for reaching other goals, not even in the name of the well-being and progress of the community as a whole. By creating man in His own image, God wished to make him share in His lordship and His glory. When He entrusted him with the task of caring for all creation, He took into account his creative intelligence and his responsible freedom....

When God turns His gaze on man, the first thing He sees and loves in him is not the deeds he succeeds in doing, but His own image, an image that confers on man the ability to know and love his own Creator, to rule over all earthly creatures and to use them for God's glory. And this is why the Church recognizes the same dignity in all human beings and the same fundamental value, regardless of any circumstantial consideration. [PA]

The mystery of the Incarnation has given a tremendous impetus to man's thought and artistic genius. Precisely by reflecting on the union of the two natures, human and divine, in the Person of the Incarnate Word, Christian thinkers have come to explain the concept of person as the unique and unrepeatable center of freedom and responsibility, whose inalienable dignity must be realized. This concept of the person has proved to be the cornerstone of any genuinely human civilization....

The great ideal of the Beatitudes remains for man—for man of every time, every place, and every culture—an incomparable source of inspiration, by the wonder it arouses and by the way it expands his capacity to be and to act, to contemplate and to create....

Faith in Christ, the Incarnate Word, leads us to see man in a new light. In a certain sense, it enables us to believe in man, created in the image and likeness of God, at once a microcosm of the world and an icon of God. [PA]

Freedom can be a risk....
If freedom does not obey the truth,
it can crush you. [YR]

Many of [today's] problems are the result of a false notion of individual freedom at work in our culture, as if one could be free only when rejecting every objective norm of conduct, refusing to assume responsibility or even refusing to put curbs on instincts and passions! Instead, true freedom implies that we are capable of choosing a good without constraint. This is the truly human way of proceeding in the choices —big and small—which life puts before us.

The fact that we are also able to choose not to act as we see we should is a necessary condition of our moral freedom. But in that case we must account for the good that we fail to do and for the evil that we commit. This sense of moral accountability needs to be reawakened if society is to survive as a civilization of justice and solidarity.

It is true that our freedom is weakened and conditioned in many ways, not least as a consequence of the mysterious and dramatic history of mankind's original rebellion against the Creator's will.... But we remain free and responsible beings who have been redeemed by Jesus Christ, and we must educate our freedom to recognize and choose what is right and good, and to reject what does not conform to the original truth concerning our nature and our destiny as God's creatures. [WB]

Freedom is not simply the absence of tyranny or oppression. Nor is freedom a license to do whatever we like. Freedom has an inner logic which distinguishes it and ennobles it: Freedom is ordered to the truth, and is fulfilled in man's quest for truth and in man's living the truth. Detached from the truth about the human person, freedom deteriorates into license in the lives of individuals and, in political life, it becomes the caprice of the most powerful and the arrogance of power. Far from being a limitation upon freedom or a threat to it, reference to the truth about the human person—a truth universally knowable through the moral law written on the hearts of all—is, in fact, the guarantor of freedom's future. [UN]

Truth—beginning with the truth of our redemption through the cross and resurrection of Jesus Christ—is the root and rule of freedom, the foundation and measure of all liberating action. [WB]

The American people possess the intelligence and will to meet the challenge of rededicating themselves with renewed vigor to fostering the truths on which this country was founded and by which it grew. Those truths are enshrined in the Declaration of Independence, the Constitution, and the Bill of Rights, and they still today receive a broad consensus among Americans. Those truths sustain values which have led people all over the world to look to America with hope and respect.

To all Americans, without exception, I present this invitation: Let us pause and reason together. To educate without a value system based on truth is to abandon young people to moral confusion, personal insecurity, and easy manipulation. No country, not even the most powerful, can endure if it deprives its own children of this essential good. Respect for the dignity and worth of every person, integrity and responsibility, as well as understanding, compassion, and solidarity toward others survive only if they are passed on in families, in schools, and through the communications media. [DS]

America has a strong tradition of respect for the individual, for human dignity and human rights.... America, you are beautiful and blessed in so many ways. But your best beauty and your richest blessing is found in the human person: in each man, woman, and child, in every immigrant, in every native-born son and daughter. The ultimate test of your greatness is the way you treat every human being, but especially the weakest and most defenseless ones. The best traditions of your land presume respect for those who cannot defend themselves.

If you want equal justice for all, and true freedom and lasting peace, then, America, defend life! All the great causes that are yours today will have meaning only to the extent that you guarantee the right to life and protect the human person. [DS]

It would be a great tragedy for the entire human family if the United States, which prides itself on its consecration to freedom, were to lose sight of the true meaning of that noble word. America: You cannot insist on the right to choose, without also insisting on the duty to choose well, the duty to choose the truth. Already there is much breakdown and pain in your own society because fundamental values essential to the well-being of individuals, families, and the entire nation are being emptied of their real content.

And yet, at the same time, throughout this land there is a great stirring, an awareness of the urgent need to recapture the ultimate meaning of life and its fundamental values. Surely by now we must be convinced that only by recognizing the primacy of moral values can we use the immense possibilities offered by science and material progress to bring about the true advancement of the human person in truth, freedom, and dignity. [WB]

The trivialization of sexuality, especially in the media, and the acceptance in some societies of a sexuality without moral restraint and without accountability, are deleterious above all to women, increasing the challenges that they face in sustaining their personal dignity and their service to life. In a society which follows this path, the temptation to use abortion as a so-called solution to the unwanted results of sexual promiscuity and irresponsibility is very strong. And here again it is the woman who bears the heaviest burden: Often left alone, or pressured into terminating the life of her child before it is born, she must then bear the burden of her conscience, which forever reminds her that she has taken the life of her child.

A radical solidarity with women requires that the underlying causes which make a child unwanted be addressed. There will never be justice, including equality, development, and peace, for women or for men, unless there is an unfailing determination to respect, serve, love, and protect every human life, at every stage and in every situation. [BE]

In the sphere of human rights, it is more appropriate than ever to ask our contemporaries to question themselves on what is mistakenly called "reproductive health." The expression contains a contradiction that distorts the very meaning of subjectivity: Actually, it includes the alleged right to abortion. Thus it denies the basic right of every human being to life, and in harming one of its members it injures the whole human race. The roots of the contradiction between the solemn affirmation of human rights and their tragic denial in practice lies in a notion of freedom which exalts the isolated individual in an absolute way, and gives no place to solidarity, openness to others, and service of them.

Recognition of someone as a human being is never based on the awareness or experience we may have of him, but by the certitude that he has an infinite value from conception, which comes to him from his relationship with God. A human being has primacy over the idea others have of him, and his existence is absolute and not relative. [MW]

May my good wishes for peace reach all the people on this [Christmas] day which celebrates the Prince of Peace. May they particularly reach families, children, women, old people, the handicapped, who are often helpless victims of selfishness and neglect by society. I ask the Lord, tiny and defenseless as He appears before us in the crib, to inspire tenderness and compassion in every heart.

Wipe away, Baby Jesus, the tears of children! Embrace the sick and the elderly! Move men to lay down their arms and to draw close in a universal embrace of peace! Invite the peoples, O merciful Jesus, to tear down the walls created by poverty and unemployment, by ignorance and indifference, by discrimination and intolerance. It is You, O divine child of Bethlehem, who save us, freeing us from sin. It is You who are the true and only Savior, whom humanity often searches for with uncertainty. God of peace, gift of peace for all of humanity: Come to live in the heart of every individual and of every family. Be our peace and joy! Amen! [CM]

Equality, as most women themselves point out, does not mean "sameness with men." This would only impoverish women and all of society, by deforming or losing the unique richness and the inherent value of femininity. In the Church's outlook, women and men have been called by the Creator to live in profound communion with one another with reciprocal knowledge and giving of self, acting together for the common good with the complementary characteristics of that which is feminine and masculine. [BE]

Where communities or countries lack basic social infrastructures and economic opportunities, women and children are the first to experience marginalization. And yet, where poverty abounds, or in the face of the devastation of conflict and war, or the tragedy of migration, forced or otherwise, it is very often women who maintain the vestiges of human dignity, defend the family, and preserve cultural and religious values. History is written almost exclusively as the narrative of men's achievements, when in fact its better part is most often molded by women's determined and persevering action for good....

How much still needs to be said and written about man's enormous debt to woman in every other realm of social and cultural progress! The Church and human society have been, and continue to be, measurelessly enriched by the unique presence and gifts of women, especially those who have consecrated themselves to the Lord and in Him have given themselves in service to others. [BE]

We must learn to read the history of other peoples without facile and partisan bias, making an effort to understand their point of view. This is a real challenge also on the level of education and culture. This is a challenge for civilization! If we agree to set out on this journey, we shall come to see that mistakes are not all on one side. We shall see how history has sometimes been presented in a distorted and even manipulated way, with tragic results.

A correct reading of history will make it easier to accept and appreciate the social, cultural, and religious differences between individuals, groups, and peoples. This is the first step towards reconciliation, since respect for differences is an inherently necessary condition for genuine relationships between individuals and between groups. The suppression of differences can result in apparent peace, but it creates a volatile situation which is in fact the prelude to fresh outbreaks of violence. [WD]

Wars, even when they "solve" the problems which cause them, do so only by leaving a wake of victims and destruction which weighs heavily upon ensuing peace negotiations. Awareness of this should encourage peoples, nations, and states once and for all to rise above the "culture of war," not only in its most detestable form—namely, the power to wage war used as an instrument of supremacy—but also in the less odious but no less destructive form of recourse to arms as an expeditious way to solve a problem. Precisely in a time such as ours, which is familiar with the most sophisticated technologies of destruction, it is urgently necessary to develop a consistent "culture of peace," which will forestall and counter the seemingly inevitable outbreaks of armed violence, including taking steps to stop the growth of the arms industry and of arms trafficking.

But even before this, the sincere desire for peace has to be translated into a firm decision to remove every obstacle to achieving peace. Here, the various religions can make an important contribution, as they have often done in the past, by speaking out against war and bravely facing the consequent risks. But are not all of us called to do still more, by drawing upon the genuine patrimony of our religious traditions? [WD]

Solidarity means taking responsibility for those in trouble. For Christians, the migrant is not merely an individual to be respected in accordance with the norms established by law, but a person whose presence challenges them and whose needs become an obligation for their responsibility. "What have you done to your brother?" (see Gn 4:9). The answer should not be limited to what is imposed by law, but should be made in the manner of solidarity.

Man, particularly if he is weak, defenseless, driven to the margins of society, is a sacrament of Christ's presence (see Mt 25:40, 45).... "I was a stranger and you welcomed me" (v. 35). It is the Church's task not only to present constantly the Lord's teaching of faith, but also to indicate its appropriate application to the various situations which the changing times continue to create. Today the illegal migrant comes before us like that "stranger" in whom Jesus asks to be recognized. To welcome him and to show him solidarity is a duty of hospitality and fidelity to Christian identity itself. [MD]

The world has yet to learn how to live with diversity.... The fact of difference, and the reality of "the other," can sometimes be felt as a burden, or even as a threat. Amplified by historic grievances and exacerbated by the manipulations of the unscrupulous, the fear of difference can lead to a denial of the very humanity of "the other," with the result that people fall into a cycle of violence in which no one is spared, not even the children....

From bitter experience, then, we know that the fear of difference, especially when it expresses itself in a narrow and exclusive nationalism which denies any rights to "the other," can lead to a true nightmare of violence and terror. And yet if we make the effort to look at matters objectively, we can see that, transcending all the differences which distinguish individuals and peoples, there is a fundamental commonality. Different cultures are but different ways of facing the question of the meaning of personal existence. And it is precisely here that we find one source of the respect which is due to every culture and every nation. Every culture is an effort to ponder the mystery of the world and in particular of the human person: It is a way of giving expression to the transcendent dimension of human life. The heart of every culture is its approach to the greatest of all mysteries: the mystery of God. [UN]

To cut oneself off from the reality of difference [between cultures]—or worse, to attempt to stamp out that difference—is to cut oneself off from the possibility of sounding the depths of the mystery of human life. The truth about man is the unchangeable standard by which all cultures are judged. But every culture has something to teach us about one or other dimension of that complex truth. Thus the difference which some find so threatening can, through respectful dialogue, become the source of a deeper understanding of the mystery of human existence. [UN]

We need to clarify the essential difference between an unhealthy form of nationalism, which teaches contempt for other nations or cultures, and patriotism, which is a proper love of one's country. True patriotism never seeks to advance the well-being of one's own nation at the expense of others. For in the end this would harm one's own nation as well: Doing wrong damages both aggressor and victim. Nationalism, particularly in its most radical forms, is thus the antithesis of true patriotism, and today we must ensure that extreme nationalism does not continue to give rise to new forms of the aberrations of totalitarianism. [UN]

The politics of nations ... can never ignore the transcendent, spiritual dimension of the human experience, and could never ignore it without harming the cause of man and the cause of human freedom. Whatever diminishes man—whatever shortens the horizon of man's aspiration to goodness—harms the cause of freedom. In order to recover our hope and our trust at the end of this century of sorrows, we must regain sight of that transcendent horizon of possibility to which the soul of man aspires. [UN]

We do not live in an irrational or meaning-less world. On the contrary, there is a moral logic which is built into human life and which makes possible dialogue between individuals and peoples. If we want a century of violent coercion to be succeeded by a century of persuasion, we must find a way to discuss the human future intelligibly. The universal moral law written on the human heart is precisely that kind of "grammar" which is needed if the world is to engage in this discussion of its future. [UN]

The third millennium is posing numerous questions to humanity ... but it also offers new and unsuspected perspectives. What will the world of the twenty-first century be like? Shall we be able to make the most of our past experiences and build peaceful coexistence in the heart of each national community and among the nations? Will the longing for freedom of so many persons and peoples of the earth be granted?

Now that the collective systems that stifled worthwhile personal or group projects seem to have been overcome, will the world be in thrall to the blind mechanisms of a kind of pitiless economic organization which takes no account of the weakest and frustrates the aspirations of the poor? ... The Church herself feels it her duty to alert the consciences of those who exercise public office to their great responsibilities in the area of politics or of the economy which is closely connected with it. [EC]

The figure of Saint Joseph recalls the urgent need to give a soul to the world of work. His life, marked by listening to God and by familiarity with Christ, appears as a harmonious synthesis of faith and life, of personal fulfillment and love for one's brothers and sisters, of daily commitment, and of trust in the future.

May his witness remind those who work that only by accepting the primacy of God and the light that comes from Christ's cross and resurrection can they fulfill the conditions of a labor worthy of man—and find in daily toil a glimmer of new life, of the new good, as if it were an announcement of "the new heavens and the new earth" in which man and the world participate precisely through the toil that goes with work. [HW]

The right to work must ... be combined with that of freedom to choose one's own activity.

These perogatives, however, must not be understood in an individualistic sense, but in relation to the vocation to service and cooperation with others. Freedom is not exercised morally without considering its relationship and reciprocity with other freedoms. These should be understood not so much as restrictions, but as conditions for the development of individual freedom, and as an exercise of the duty to contribute to the growth of society as a whole.

Thus work is primarily a right because it is a duty arising from man's social relations. It expresses man's vocation to service and solidarity. [HW]

The special place of human beings in all that God made lies in their being given a share in God's own concern and providence for the whole of creation. The Creator has entrusted the world to us, as a gift and as a responsibility. He who is eternal Providence, the One who guides the entire universe towards its final destiny, made us in His image and likeness, so that we too should become "providence"—a wise and intelligent providence, guiding human development and the development of the world along the path of harmony with the Creator's will, and the well-being of the human family and the fulfillment of each individual's transcendent calling. [YD]

Young people are especially sensitive to the beauty of nature, and contemplating it inspires them spiritually. However, it must be a genuine contemplation. A contemplation which fails to reveal the face of a personal, intelligent, free, and loving Father, but which discerns merely the dim figure of an impersonal divinity or some cosmic force, does not suffice. We must not confuse the Creator with His creation. The creature does not have life of itself, but from God.

In discovering God's greatness, man discovers the unique position he holds in the visible world: "You have made him little less than the angels, and crowned him with glory and honor. You have given him rule over the works of your hands, putting all things under his feet" (Ps 8:6-7, NAB).

Yes, the contemplation of nature reveals not only the Creator, but also the human being's role in the world which He created. With faith it reveals the greatness of our dignity as creatures created in His image. In order to have life and have it abundantly, in order to re-establish the original harmony of creation, we must respect this divine image in all of creation, especially in human life itself. [YD]

Technology that pollutes can also cleanse, production that amasses can also distribute justly, on the condition that the ethic of respect for life and human dignity, for the rights of today's generations and those to come, prevails.

This requires firm points of reference and inspiration: a clear knowledge of creation as a work of God's provident wisdom and the awareness of human dignity and responsibility in the plan of creation. [EH]

It is by looking at the face of God that man can brighten the face of the earth and ensure environmental hospitality for man today and tomorrow. [EH]

5
HELP THE POOR

Then the righteous will answer him, "Lord, when did we see thee hungry and feed thee, or thirsty and give thee drink? And when did we see thee a stranger and welcome thee, or naked and clothe thee? And when did we see thee sick or in prison and visit thee?" And the King will answer them, "Truly, I say to you, as you did it to one of the least of these my brethren, you did it to me."

MATTHEW 25:37-40, RSV

The great value of each person ... Christ comes to us in the poor ... detachment from material goods ... our brother's keeper ... consumerism, hedonism, indifference ... the right to housing ... charity and hope ... charity and evangelism ... the poverty of mental illness ... poverty of the spirit ... friends to the friendless ... poverty and peace

The Church bears witness that every person is more valuable than all the gold in the world. [CU]

It is from the love of God that Christians learn to help the needy and to share with them their own material and spiritual goods. Such concern not only provides those experiencing hardship with material help but also represents an opportunity for the spiritual growth of the giver, who finds in it an incentive to become detached from worldly goods. But there is a higher motivation which Christ indicated to us by His own example when He said: "The Son of man has nowhere to lay his head" (Mt 8:20, RSV).

By these words the Lord wished to show His total openness to His heavenly Father, whose will He was determined to carry out without letting Himself be hindered by the possession of worldly goods. For there is always a danger that earthly realities will take the place of God in the human heart.... As Christians, we must direct our entire lives to Him, for we know that in this world we have no fixed abode: "Our commonwealth is in heaven" (Phil 3:20, RSV). [SL]

Poverty is driving masses of people to the margins of society, or even worse, to extinction. For too many people war has become a harsh everyday reality. A society interested only in material and ephemeral goods is tending to marginalize those who are not useful to its purposes.

Faced with situations like these, involving real human tragedies, some prefer simply to close their eyes, taking refuge in indifference. Theirs is the attitude of Cain: "Am I my brother's keeper?" (Gn 4:9, RSV). But the Church has the duty to remind everyone of God's severe admonishment: "What have you done? The voice of your brother's blood is crying to me from the ground!" (Gn 4:10, RSV).

When so many of our brothers and sisters are suffering, we cannot remain indifferent! Their distress appeals to our conscience, the inner sanctuary where we come face to face with ourselves and with God. How can we fail to see that, to different degrees, we are all involved in this revision of life to which God is calling us? We all need forgiveness from God and from our neighbor. Therefore we must all be ready to forgive and to ask forgiveness. [WD]

The crowds of starving people—children, women, the elderly, immigrants, refugees, the unemployed—raise to us their cry of suffering. They implore us, hoping to be heard. How can we not open our ears and our hearts and start to make available those five loaves and two fish which God has put into our hands? If each one of us contributes something, we can all do something for them. Of course this will require sacrifices, which call for a deep inner conversion. Certainly it will involve changing our exaggerated consumerist behavior, combating hedonism, resisting attitudes of indifference and the tendency to disregard our personal responsibilities. [GT]

More than 800 million people still suffer from malnutrition, and ... it is often difficult to find immediate solutions for improving these tragic situations. Nevertheless, we must seek them together so that we will no longer have, side by side, the starving and the wealthy, the very poor and the very rich, those who lack the necessary means and others who lavishly waste them. Such contrasts between poverty and wealth are intolerable for humanity. [FS]

Ensuring a suitable habitat for everyone is demanded by the respect owed to every human being and, therefore, is a measure of civilization and the condition for a peaceful, fraternal society. By virtue of his human dignity, every person must be guaranteed a lodging which offers not only physical shelter but a suitable place for satisfying his social, cultural, and spiritual needs.

May the Blessed Virgin help all to overcome selfish temptations and to open their hearts to the needs of their brothers and sisters. If states have precise duties in providing housing, much also depends on the sensitivity of private individuals. Moreover, how can political guidelines inspired by justice and solidarity be promoted, if these values are not woven into the fabric of society as a whole? I hope that everyone—particularly those who appeal to the gospel of Christ—will develop a greater sensitivity to the concrete, urgent issue of the right to housing. [HS]

Distinguishing between the necessary and the dispensable enables each person to be more open and more generous to his needy brothers and sisters, to purify his personal relationship with money, and to moderate his attachment to the good things of this world. [CU]

In all the members of the Church and in all people of goodwill, the Jubilee must foster an awareness of the need to cooperate in meeting the challenge of sharing, of the equitable distribution of goods, and of joining forces. In this way everyone will contribute to the building up of a more just and fraternal society, the premise of the Kingdom, because love is a witness to the Kingdom to come, and it alone can radically transform the world. [CU]

Charity restores hope to the poor, who realize they are truly loved by God. [CU]

Those who practice charity carry out a profound work of evangelization.... Sometimes, action in communion is more eloquent than any teaching; and actions joined to words give particularly effective witness. The disciples of the Lord will recall that serving the poor and suffering is serving Christ, who is the light of the world. By living daily in the love that comes from Him, the faithful help spread light in the world. [CU]

Charity goes beyond justice, for it is an invitation to go beyond the order of mere equity to the order of love and self-giving. [CU]

Christ not only took pity on the sick and healed many of them, restoring health to both their minds and their bodies; His compassion also led Him to identify with them. He declares: "I was sick and you visited me" (Mt 25:36, RSV). The disciples of the Lord, precisely because they were able to see the image of the suffering Christ in all people marked by sickness, opened their hearts to them, spending themselves in various forms of assistance.

Well, Christ took all human suffering on Himself, even mental illness. Yes, even this affliction, which perhaps seems the most absurd and incomprehensible, configures the sick person to Christ and gives him a share in His redeeming passion.

Thus ... whoever suffers from mental illness always bears God's image and likeness in himself, as does every human being. In addition, he always has the inalienable right not only to be considered as an image of God and therefore as a person, but also to be treated as such....

Our actions must show that mental illness does not create insurmountable distances, nor prevent relations of true Christian charity with those who are its victims. Indeed, it should inspire a particularly attentive attitude towards these people who are fully entitled to belong to the category of the poor to whom the kingdom of heaven belongs (see Mt 5:3). [HC]

America has a reputation the world over, a reputation of power, prestige, and wealth. But not everyone here is powerful; not everyone here is rich. In fact, America's sometimes extravagant affluence often conceals much hardship and poverty.

From the viewpoint of the kingdom of God we must therefore ask a very basic question: Have the people living [here] lost sight of the blessings which belong to the poor in spirit? In the midst of the magnificent scientific and technological civilization of which America is proud, ... is there room for the mystery of God? That mystery which is "revealed to the merest children" (see Mt 11:25); the mystery of the Father and the Son in the unity of the Holy Spirit, the mystery of the divine love which is the source of everything? Is there room for the revelation of life—that transcendent life which Christ brings us at the price of His cross and through the victory of His resurrection? [AR]

Become friends to those who have no friends.
Become family to those who have no family.
Become community to those who have no community. [YR]

"Nation shall not lift up sword against nation, neither shall they learn war any more" (Is 2:4, RSV). These are the words of the prophet Isaiah, who proclaimed the dawn of universal peace. But according to the prophet, this peace will come about ... only when "they shall beat their swords into plowshares, and their spears into pruning hooks." For only when people consider the struggle against hunger as a priority, and are committed to providing everyone with the means of gaining their daily bread instead of amassing weapons, will conflicts and wars come to an end and humanity be able to set forth on a lasting journey of peace. [FA]

I would like to call attention to the threat to peace posed by poverty, especially when it becomes destitution. There are millions of men, women, and children suffering every day from hunger, insecurity, and marginalization. These situations constitute a grave affront to human dignity and contribute to social instability....

If you want peace, reach out to the poor! May rich and poor recognize that they are brothers and sisters. May they share what they have with one another as children of the one God who loves everyone, who wills the good of everyone, and who offers to everyone the gift of peace! [PP]

6
BE A DOMESTIC CHURCH

Blessed is every one who fears the Lord, who walks in his ways! You shall eat the fruit of the labor of your hands; you shall be happy, and it shall be well with you. Your wife will be like a fruitful vine within your house; your children will be like olive shoots around your table. Lo, thus shall the man be blessed who fears the Lord.

PSALM 128:1-4, RSV

The church in the home ... parents as models ... honoring marriage and family ... cooperating in God's creative work ... conjugal love as the gift of self ... women's roles in the family ... the family as communion ... challenges to the family ... marriage as sacred reality ... families called to holiness ... family unity ... family prayer and worship ... the special gifts of children and youth

God comes to us in the things we know best and can verify most easily, the things of our everyday life, apart from which we cannot understand ourselves. [FR 12]

Catholic parents must learn to form their family as a "domestic Church," a Church in the home as it were, where God is honored, His law is respected, prayer is a normal event, virtue is transmitted by word and example, and everyone shares the hopes, the problems, and sufferings of everyone else. All this is not to advocate a return to some outdated style of living: It is to return to the roots of human development and human happiness! [MF]

Little children very soon learn about life. They watch and imitate the behavior of adults. They rapidly learn love and respect for others, but they also quickly absorb the poison of violence and hatred. Family experiences strongly condition the attitudes which children will assume as adults. Consequently, if the family is the place where children first encounter the world, the family must be for children the first school of peace. [MF]

The gospel of the Kingdom of God is open to every aspect of earthly progress which helps people to discover and enter the space of divine life, the space of eternal salvation. This is the work of the Church; this is the work which the Holy Spirit will accomplish through all of us, if only we will heed the truth He reveals and be confirmed in goodness!

In practical terms, this truth tells us that there can be no life worthy of the human person without a culture—and a legal system—that honors and defends marriage and the family. The well-being of individuals and communities depends on the healthy state of the family....

Society must strongly reaffirm the right of the child to grow up in a family in which, as far as possible, both parents are present. Fathers of families must accept their full share of responsibility for the lives and upbringing of their children. Both parents must spend time with their children, and be personally interested in their moral and religious education. Children need not only material support from their parents, but more importantly a secure, affectionate, and morally correct family environment. [AR]

Those who have the gift of faith know that there is a creative act of God at every person's origin, a plan of love that awaits fulfillment. This fundamental truth, accessible even within the limited power of reason, permits one to catch a glimpse of the very lofty mission inscribed in human sexuality: It is, in fact, called to cooperate with the creative power of God. [GE]

Conjugal love is the loftiest and most beautiful expression of human relations and self-giving, for it is essentially a desire for mutual growth. In this encounter based on reciprocal love, each is recognized for what he is and is called to express his personal talents and achieve his potential. The logic of the sincere gift of self is a source of joy, help, and understanding. [MW]

No response to women's issues can ignore women's role in the family or take lightly the fact that every new life is entrusted to the protection and care of the woman carrying it in her womb. In order to respect this natural order of things, it is necessary to counter the misconception that the role of motherhood is oppressive to women, and that a commitment to her family, particularly to her children, prevents a woman from reaching personal fulfillment, and women as a whole from having an influence in society. It is a disservice not only to children, but also to women and society itself, when a woman is made to feel guilty for wanting to remain in the home and nurture and care for her children.

A mother's presence in the family, so critical to the stability and growth of that basic unity of society, should instead be recognized, applauded, and supported in every possible way. By the same token society needs to, and ought to, strive for a situation in which they will not be forced by economic circumstances to move away from the home in search of work. [BE]

The bond that unites a family is not only a matter of natural kinship or of shared life and experience. It is essentially a holy and religious bond. Marriage and the family are sacred realities. The sacredness of Christian marriage consists in the fact that in God's plan the marriage covenant between a man and a woman becomes the image and symbol of the covenant which unites God and his people (see Hos 2:19-20; Jer 3:6-13; Is 54:5-10). It is the sign of Christ's love for his Church (see Eph 5:32).

Because God's love is faithful and irrevocable, so those who have been married in Christ are called to remain faithful to each other forever. Did not Jesus Himself say to us: "What therefore God has joined together, let not man put asunder" (Mt 19:6, RSV)? Contemporary society has a special need of the witness of couples who persevere in their union as an eloquent, even if sometimes suffering, sign in our human condition of the steadfastness of God's love. Day after day Christian married couples are called to open their hearts ever more to the Holy Spirit, whose power never fails and who enables them to love each other as Christ has loved us. [WB]

As Saint Paul writes to the Galatians, "the fruit of the spirit is love, joy, peace, patient endurance, kindness, generosity, faith, mildness, and chastity" (Gal 5:22-23, NAB). All of this constitutes the rule of life and the program of personal development of Christian couples. And each Christian community has a great responsibility to sustain couples in their love.

From such love Christian families are born. In them children are welcomed as a splendid gift of God's goodness, and they are educated in the essential values of human life, learning above all that "man is more precious for what he is than for what he has" (see *Gaudium et spes*, n. 35). [WB]

Christian families exist to form a communion of persons in love. As such, the Church and the family are each in its own way living representations in human history of the eternal loving communion of the three persons of the Most Holy Trinity. In fact, the family is called the Church in miniature, "the domestic church," a particular expression of the Church through the human experience of love and common life. Like the Church, the family ought to be a place where the gospel is transmitted and from which the gospel radiates to other families and to the whole of society. [WB]

In America and throughout the world, the family is being shaken to its roots. The consequences for individuals and society in personal and collective instability and unhappiness are incalculable. Yet it is heartening to know that in the face of this extraordinary challenge many Christians are committing themselves to the defense and support of family life.... This is a field in which there must be the maximum collaboration among all who confess Jesus Christ.

So often the pressures of modern living separate husbands and wives from one another, threatening their life-long interdependence in love and fidelity. Can we also not be concerned about the impact of cultural pressures upon relations between the generations, upon parental authority and the transmission of sacred values? Our Christian conscience should be deeply concerned about the way in which sins against love and against life are often presented as examples of "progress" and emancipation. Most often, are they not simply the age-old forms of selfishness dressed up in a new language and presented in a new cultural framework? [WB]

Man and woman, called to live in the process of cosmic creation, appear on the threshold of their own vocation, bringing with them the ability to procreate in collaboration with God, who directly creates the soul of each new human being. Through mutual knowledge and love, and at the same time through physical union, they will call to life beings resembling themselves and, like them, created "in the image and likeness of God." They will give life to their own children, just as they received it from their parents.

This is the truth, both simple and great, about the family, as it is presented in the pages of the Book of Genesis and of the gospel: In God's plan, marriage—indissoluble marriage—is the basis of a healthy and responsible family. [MF]

Parents and families of the whole world, let me say to you: God calls you to holiness! He Himself has chosen you "before the creation of the world," Saint Paul tells us, to "be holy and blameless before him … through Jesus Christ" (Eph 1:4, 5, RSV). He loves you passionately, He desires your happiness, but He wants you to be always able to *combine fidelity with happiness, because one cannot exist without the other.* Do not let a hedonistic mentality, ambition, and selfishness enter your homes. Be generous with God….

The family, as an intimate community of life and love, is at the service of the Church and of society. The mutual gift of self, blessed by God and imbued with faith, hope, and love, will enable both spouses to achieve perfection and sanctification. In other words, it will serve as the sanctifying center of one's own family and of spreading the work of evangelizing the whole Christian home. [MF]

e bearers of peace and joy within the family. Grace elevates and perfects love, and with it, grants you the indispensable family virtues of humility, the spirit of service and sacrifice, parental and filial affection, respect and mutual understanding.... May the spirit of the Holy Family of Nazareth reign in all Christian homes! [MF]

Jesus prays to His heavenly Father that all may be one (see Jn 17:21): This prayer comes to His lips the day before His passion. But it is a prayer which He already carries in Himself at the moment of His birth: Father, that "they may be one even as we are one" (Jn 17:22, RSV).

Was He not praying at that moment also for the unity of human families? He was certainly praying above all for the unity of the Church; but the family, sustained by a special sacrament, is the vital cell of the Church; indeed, according to the teaching of the Fathers, it is a little domestic church. So Jesus prayed from the very time of His coming into the world that all who believe in Him might give expression to their communion, starting with the profound unity of God's plan for conjugal love from which the family takes its origin (see Mt 19:4-6).

We can therefore hold that Jesus prayed for the sacred and fundamental unity of every family. He prayed for the union of God's children in truth and charity. Having given the sincere gift of Himself in coming into this world, He prayed that all people, in founding a family, would become, for the good of that family, a sincere mutual gift of self: husbands and wives, parents and children, and all the generations which make up the family, each individual making his or her own particular contribution. [CM]

For Christian families, the Sunday assembly is one of the most outstanding expressions of their identity and their ministry as domestic churches, when parents share with their children at the one table of the Word and of the Bread of Life. [DD]

Through Sunday rest, daily concerns and tasks can find their proper perspective: The material things about which we worry give way to spiritual values; in a moment of encounter and less-pressured exchange, we see the true face of the people with whom we live. Even the beauties of nature—too often marred by the desire to exploit, which turns against man himself—can be rediscovered and enjoyed to the full. [DD]

The Church prays for the Christian family and educates the family to live in generous accord with the priestly gift and role received from Christ the high priest. In effect, the baptismal priesthood of the faithful exercised in the sacrament of marriage constitutes the basis of a priestly vocation and mission for the spouses and family by which their daily lives are transformed into "spiritual sacrifices acceptable to God through Jesus Christ" (1 Pt 2:5, RSV). This transformation is achieved not only by celebrating the Eucharist and the other sacraments and through offering themselves to the glory of God, but also through a life of prayer, through prayerful dialogue with the Father, through Jesus Christ, in the Holy Spirit. [FC]

Family prayer has for its very own object family life itself, which in all its varying circumstances is seen as a call from God and lived as a filial response to his call. Joys and sorrows, hopes and disappointments, births and birthday celebrations, wedding anniversaries of the parents, departures, separations, and homecomings, important and far-reaching decisions, the death of those who are dear ... all of these mark God's loving intervention in the family's history. They should be seen as suitable moments for thanksgiving, for petition, for trusting abandonment of the family into the hands of their common Father in heaven. The dignity and responsibility of the Christian family as the domestic church can be achieved only with God's unceasing aid, which will surely be granted if it is humbly and trustingly petitioned in prayer. [FC]

By reason of their dignity and mission, Christian parents have the specific responsibility of educating their children in prayer, introducing them to gradual discovery of the mystery of God and to personal dialogue with Him.... The concrete example and living witness of parents is fundamental and irreplaceable in educating their children to pray. Only by praying together with their children can a father and mother—exercising their royal priesthood—penetrate the innermost depths of their children's hearts and leave an impression that the future events in their lives will not be able to efface. [FC]

Family, O Holy Family ... guide with your example the families of the whole earth!... Son of God, who came among us in the warmth of the family, grant that all families may grow in love and work together for the good of all humanity through the commitment of faithful and fruitful unity, through respect for life and the quest for fraternal solidarity with everyone. Teach them therefore to renounce selfishness, deceit, and the unscrupulous quest for their own gain. Help them to develop the immense resources of heart and mind, which increase when it is You who inspire them. [CM]

How important children are in the eyes of Jesus! We could even say that the gospel is full of the truth about children. The whole of the gospel could actually be read as the "Gospel of children." What does it mean that "unless you turn and become like children, you will not enter the kingdom of heaven" (Mt 18:3, RSV)? Is not Jesus pointing to children as models even for grown-ups? In children there is something that must never be missing in people who want to enter the kingdom of heaven. People who are destined to go to heaven are simple like children, and like children are full of trust, rich in goodness, and pure. Only people of this sort can find in God a Father and, thanks to Jesus, can become in their own turn children of God. {CH}

Jesus and His mother often choose children and give them important tasks for the life of the Church and of humanity.... The Redeemer of humanity seems to share with them His concern for others: for parents, for other boys and girls. He eagerly awaits their prayers. What enormous power the prayer of children has! This becomes a model for grown-ups themselves: praying with simple and complete trust means praying as children pray.

Dear young friends, it is to your prayers that I want to entrust the problems of your own families and of all the families in the world. And not only this: I also have other intentions to ask you to pray for. The pope counts very much on your prayers. We must pray together and pray hard, that humanity, made up of billions of human beings, may become more and more the family of God and able to live in peace.... Dear boys and girls, take upon yourselves the duty of praying for peace.

You know this well: Love and harmony build peace, hatred and violence destroy it. You instinctively turn away from hatred and are attracted by love: for this reason the pope is certain that you will not refuse his request, but that you will join in his prayer for peace in the world with the same enthusiasm with which you pray for peace and harmony in your own families. [CH]

It is to you, young friends, without distinction of language, race, or nationality, that I say: Praise the name of the Lord! And since people must praise God first of all with their own lives, do not forget what the twelve-year-old Jesus said to His mother and to Joseph in the Temple in Jerusalem: "Did you not know that I must be in My Father's house?" (Lk 2:49, RSV).

People praise God by following the voice of their own calling. God calls every person, and His voice makes itself heard even in the hearts of children: He calls people to live in marriage or to be priests; He calls them to the consecrated life or perhaps to work on the missions.... Who can say? Pray dear boys and girls, that you will find out what your calling is, and that you will then follow it generously. Praise the name of the Lord! [CH]

In my pastoral visits to the Church in every part of the world I have been deeply moved by the almost universal conditions of difficulty in which young people grow up and live. Too many sufferings are visited upon them by natural calamities, famines, epidemics, by economic and political crises, by the atrocities of wars. And where material conditions are at least adequate, other obstacles arise, not the least of which is the breakdown of family values and stability. In developed countries, a serious moral crisis is already affecting the lives of many young people, leaving them adrift, often without hope, and conditioned to look only for instant gratification.

Yet everywhere there are young men and women deeply concerned about the world around them, ready to give the best of themselves in service to others and particularly sensitive to life's transcendent meaning. But how do we help them? Only by instilling a high moral vision can a society ensure that its young people are given the possibility to mature as free and intelligent human beings, endowed with a robust sense of responsibility to the common good, capable of working with others to create a community and a nation with a strong moral fiber. America was built on such a vision. [DS]

As we look toward the year 2000, how can we fail to think of the young? What is being held up to them? A society of "things" and not of "persons." The right to do as they will from their earliest years, without any constraint, provided it is "safe." The unreserved gift of self, mastery of one's instincts, the sense of responsibility—these are notions considered as belonging to another age....

We may well fear that tomorrow those same people, once they have reached adulthood, will demand an explanation from today's leaders for having deprived them of reasons for living because they failed to teach them the duties incumbent upon being endowed with intelligence and free will. [LC]

7
SHARE
FAITH

For, "every one who calls upon the name of the Lord will be saved." But how are men to call upon him in whom they have not believed? And how are they to believe in him of whom they have never heard?

ROMANS 10:13-14, RSV

No shame, no fear in evangelism ... faith leads us beyond ourselves ... the gospel is power ... called to be witnesses and missionaries ... faith and mission ... mission as duty and privilege ... radiating Jesus ... prophets of life ... the unavoidable cross ... witness to true freedom ... witness to moral truth ... the witness of sacred art ... people are seeking ... engage in dialogue ... the witness of the martyrs

What does Christ ask of you? Jesus asks you not to be ashamed of Him and to commit yourselves to proclaiming Him to your peers…. Do not be afraid, because Jesus is with you! Do not be afraid of getting lost: The more you give of yourselves, the more you will find yourselves! [YR]

The apostles ask Jesus: "Increase our faith" (Lk 17:5, RSV). This must be our constant prayer. Faith is always demanding, because faith leads us beyond ourselves. It leads us directly to God. Faith also imparts a vision of life's purpose and stimulates us to action. The gospel of Jesus Christ is not a private opinion, a remote spiritual ideal, or a mere program for personal growth. The gospel is the power which can transform the world!

The gospel is no abstraction: It is the living Person of Jesus Christ, the Word of God, the reflection of the Father's glory (see Heb 1:3), the Incarnate Son who reveals the deepest meaning of our humanity and the noble destiny to which the whole human family is called. Christ has commanded us to let the light of the gospel shine forth in our service to society. How can we profess faith in God's Word, and then refuse to let it inspire and direct our thinking, our activity, our decisions, and our responsibilities toward one another? [OP]

"But you shall receive power when the Holy Spirit has come upon you; and you shall be my witnesses in Jerusalem and in all Judea and Samaria and to the end of the earth" (Acts 1:8, RSV). On the threshold of the third millennium, the Lord Jesus repeats with force to the whole Church those same words He spoke one day to the apostles before the Ascension, words which express the essence of the Christian vocation.

Who, in fact, is the Christian? A person whom Christ "has made His own" (see Phil 3:12) and who therefore longs to make Him known and loved everywhere, "to the end of the earth." The faith spurs us to be missionaries, His witnesses. If this does not occur, it means that our faith is still incomplete, partial, and immature. [MS]

Faith and mission go hand in hand: The stronger and deeper the faith, the more we will feel the need to communicate, share, and witness to it. If, on the contrary, it weakens, missionary ardor wanes and the ability to witness loses its vigor. This has always been the case in the Church's history: A loss of vitality in the missionary impulse has always been the symptom of a faith crisis. Does this not happen because of a lack of deep conviction that faith is strengthened when it is given to others, that it is precisely by proclaiming and bearing witness to Christ that we find new enthusiasm and discover how to live a more evangelical life? [MS]

Mission is the surest antidote to the crisis of faith. Through missionary commitment, each member of the people of God invigorates his own identity, fully understanding that unless we are witnesses, we cannot be authentic Christians. [MS]

Incorporated into the Church by baptism, every Christian is called to be a missionary and witness. This is the Lord's explicit mandate. The Holy Spirit sends every baptized person to proclaim and bear witness to Christ to all nations: a *duty* then and a *privilege*, since it is an invitation to cooperate with God for the salvation of each individual and all humanity. Indeed, we have been granted "this grace … to preach to the Gentiles the unsearchable riches of Christ" (Eph 3:8, RSV).

Just as the Spirit transformed the first band of disciples into courageous apostles of the Lord and enlightened preachers of His Word, He continues to prepare witnesses to the gospel in our times. [MS]

If we are truly docile to the action of the Spirit, we will succeed in reflecting and radiating to others the mystery of love that dwells within us (see Jn 14:23). We are its witnesses. Witnesses of shining, integral faith; of active, patient, and kindly charity (see 1 Cor 13:4); of service for the many forms of poverty experienced by the contemporary man. Witnesses of the hope that does not disappoint and of the deep communion which reflects the life of God the Trinity, of obedience and the cross. In short, witnesses of holiness, "people of the Beatitudes," called to be perfect as the heavenly Father is perfect (see Mt 5:48). [MS]

Such is the identity of the Christian witness: He is a copy, a sign, a living radiance of Jesus. [MS]

I ask you young people, who naturally and instinctively make your love of life the horizon of your
dreams and the rainbow of your hopes, to become
prophets of life. Be such by your words and deeds,
rebelling against the civilization of selfishness that often
considers the human person a means rather than an end,
sacrificing its dignity and feelings in the name of mere
profit. Do so by concretely helping those who need you
and who perhaps, without your help, would be tempted
to resign themselves to despair. [YP]

The identity of the Christian as witness is marked by the unavoidable and distinctive presence of the cross. There can be no authentic witness without it. Indeed, the cross is the necessary condition for all who have firmly decided to follow the Lord: "If any man would come after me, let him deny himself and take up his cross daily and follow me" (Lk 9:23, RSV). All the witnesses of God and Christ, beginning with the apostles, have known persecution because of Him: "If they persecuted me, they will persecute you" (Jn 15:20, RSV). This is the legacy which Jesus left to His followers and which each one must accept and incarnate in his own life. Golgotha is the only way to the resurrection.

The cross, in fact, is the imitation of Christ in faithful witness and patient and persevering daily work. The cross is swimming against the tide, making decisions according to God's commandments despite misunderstanding, unpopularity, marginalization; the cross is the prophetic denunciation of injustice, of trampled freedoms, of violated rights; it is having to live where the Church is most opposed, obstructed, and persecuted. [MS]

Catholics of America! Always be guided by the truth—by the truth about God who created and redeemed us, and by the truth about the human person, made in the image and likeness of God and destined for a glorious fulfillment in the kingdom to come. Always be convincing witnesses to the truth. Stir into a flame the gift of God that has been bestowed upon you in baptism (see 2 Tm 1:6). Light your nation—light the world—with the power of that flame! Amen. [OP]

Christian witness takes different forms at different moments in the life of a nation. Sometimes, witnessing to Christ will mean drawing out of a culture the full meaning of its noblest intentions, a fullness that is revealed in Christ. At other times, witnessing to Christ means challenging that culture, especially when the truth about the human person is under assault.

America has always wanted to be a land of the free. Today, the challenge facing America is to find freedom's fulfillment in the truth: the truth that is intrinsic to human life created in God's image and likeness, the truth that can be known by reason and can therefore form the basis of a profound and universal dialogue among people about the direction they must give to their lives and their activities. [OP]

One hundred thirty years ago, President Abraham Lincoln asked whether a nation "conceived in liberty and dedicated to the proposition that all men are created equal" could "long endure." President Lincoln's question is no less a question for the present generation of Americans. Democracy cannot be sustained without a shared commitment to certain moral truths about the human person and human community. The basic question before a democratic society is: "How ought we to live together?"

In seeking an answer to this question, can society exclude moral truth and moral reasoning? Can the biblical wisdom which played such a formative part in the very founding of your country be excluded from that debate? Would not doing so mean that America's founding documents no longer have any defining content, but are only the formal dressing of changing opinion? Would not doing so mean that tens of millions of Americans could no longer offer the contribution of their deepest convictions to the formation of public policy?

Surely it is important for America that the moral truths which make freedom possible should be passed on to each new generation. Every generation of Americans needs to know that freedom consists not in doing what we like, but in having the right to do what we ought. [OP]

To believe it possible to know a universally valid truth is in no way to encourage intolerance. On the contrary, it is the essential condition for sincere and authentic dialogue between persons. On this basis alone is it possible to overcome divisions and to journey together toward full truth, walking those paths known only to the Spirit of the risen Lord. [FR 92]

People seek an absolute which might give to all their searching a meaning and an answer—something ultimate, which might serve as the ground of all things. In other words, they seek a final explanation, a supreme value, which refers to nothing beyond itself and which puts an end to all questioning. Hypotheses may fascinate, but they do not satisfy. Whether we admit it or not, there comes for everyone the moment when personal existence must be anchored to a truth recognized as final, a truth which confers a certitude no longer open to doubt. [FR 27]

By virtue of the Spirit's presence and action, the good elements found in the various religions mysteriously prepare hearts to receive the full Revelation of God in Jesus Christ.... The attitude of the Church and of individual Christians toward other religions is marked by sincere respect, profound sympathy, and, when possible and appropriate, cordial collaboration. This does not mean forgetting that Jesus Christ is the one Mediator and Savior of the human race. Nor does it mean lessening our missionary efforts, to which we are bound in obedience to the risen Lord's command: "Go therefore and make disciples of all nations, baptizing them in the name of the Father and of the Son and of the Holy Spirit" (Mt 28:19, RSV)....

Far from opposing the proclamation of the gospel, our attitude prepares it, as we await the times appointed by the Lord's mercy.... May the Spirit of truth and love ... guide us on the paths of the proclamation of Jesus Christ and of the dialogue of peace and brotherhood with the followers of all religions! [OR 9-16-98]

Christ needs you to enlighten the world and to show it the path to life. The challenge is to make the Church's "yes" to life concrete and effective. The struggle will be long, and it needs each one of you. Place your intelligence, your talents, your enthusiasm, your compassion, and your fortitude at the service of life! Have no fear. The outcome of the battle for life is already decided, even though the struggle goes on against great odds and with much suffering.... The paradox of the Christian message is this: Christ—the Head—has already conquered sin and death. Christ in his Body—the pilgrim People of God—continually suffers the onslaught of the evil one and all the evil of which sinful humanity is capable.

At this stage of history, the liberating message of the Gospel of Life has been put into your hands. And the mission of proclaiming it to the ends of the earth is now passing to your generation. Like the great apostle Paul, you too must feel the full urgency of the task: "Woe to me if I do not evangelize" (1 Cor 9:16).

Woe to you if you do not succeed in defending life. The Church needs your energies, your enthusiasm, your youthful ideals, in order to make the Gospel of Life penetrate the fabric of society, transforming people's hearts and the structures of society in order to create a civilization of true justice and love. [CC]

Now more than ever, in a world that is often without light and without the courage of noble ideals, people need the fresh, vital spirituality of the gospel. Do not be afraid to go out on the streets and into public places, like the first apostles who preached Christ and the Good News of salvation in the squares of cities, towns, and villages. This is no time to be ashamed of the gospel. It is the time to preach it from the rooftops. Do not be afraid to break out of comfortable and routine modes of living, in order to take up the challenge of making Christ known in the modern metropolis. It is you who must "go out into the by-roads" and invite everyone you meet to the banquet which God has prepared for His people.

The gospel must not be kept hidden because of fear or indifference. It was never meant to be hidden away in private. It has to be put on a stand so that people may see its light and give praise to our heavenly Father.

Jesus went in search of the men and women of His time. He engaged them in an open and truthful dialogue, whatever their condition. As the Good Samaritan of the human family, He came close to people to heal them of their sins and of the wounds which life inflicts, and to bring them back to the Father's house. [CC]

The Church asks you to go, in the power of the Holy Spirit, to those who are near and those who are far away. Share with them the freedom you have found in Christ. People thirst for genuine inner freedom. They yearn for the life which Christ came to give in abundance. The world at the approach of a new millennium, for which the whole Church is preparing, is like a field ready for the harvest. Christ needs laborers ready to work in His vineyard. May you ... not fail Him. In your hands, carry the cross of Christ. On your lips, the words of Life. In your hearts, the saving grace of the Lord. [CC]

L ike Mary, you must not be afraid to allow the Holy Spirit to help you become intimate friends of Christ. Like Mary, you must put aside any fear, in order to take Christ into the world in whatever you do—in marriage, as single people in the world, as students, as workers, as professional people. Christ wants to go to many places in the world, and to enter many hearts, through you. [NY]

Engage in dialogue in order to proclaim the Word of God. Dialogue is the method of your mission: a dialogue that first of all demands a meeting on the level of personal relations and that seeks to bring the interlocutors out of their isolation, their mutual mistrust, in order to create mutual esteem and sympathy. A dialogue that demands a meeting on the level of seeking the truth; and again, on the level of action, which tries to establish the conditions for collaboration on concrete objectives of service to one's neighbor. A dialogue that requires a Christian to be convinced of the truth, to be clearly aware that we are witnesses to Christ—the Way, the Truth, and the Life. [YR]

Just as Mary visited Elizabeth, so too you are called to "visit" the needs of the poor, the hungry, the homeless, those who are alone or ill; for example, those suffering from AIDS. You are called to stand up for life! To respect and defend the mystery of life always and everywhere, including the lives of unborn babies, giving real help and encouragement to mothers in difficult situations. You are called to work and pray against abortion, against violence of all kinds, including the violence done against women's and children's dignity through pornography. Stand up for the life of the aged and the handicapped, against attempts to promote assisted suicide and euthanasia! Stand up for marriage and family life! Stand up for purity! Resist the pressures and temptations of a world that too often tries to ignore a most fundamental truth: that every life is a gift from God our Creator, and that we must give an account to God of how we use it either for good or evil. [NY]

Jesus Christ: the Way, the Truth, and the Life (see Jn 14:6). The way of Christ is the virtuous, fruitful, and peaceful life as children of God and as brothers and sisters in the same human family. The truth of Christ is the eternal truth of God, who has revealed Himself to us not only in the created world, but also through Sacred Scripture, and especially in and through His Son, Jesus Christ, the Word made flesh. And the life of Christ is the life of grace, that free gift of God which is a created share in His own life and which enables us to live forever in His love.

When Christians are truly convinced of this, their lives are transformed. This transformation results not only in a credible and compelling witness, but also in an urgent and effective communication ... of a living faith which paradoxically increases as it is shared. [WC]

Humanity's future depends on the responsible fulfillment of persons who rely on the truth and whose lives are enlightened by lofty moral principles which enable their hearts to love to the point of sacrifice. The model of such a man, a loving servant, is Jesus Christ. This is the Church's constant proclamation to the world: Jesus Christ, the same yesterday, today, and forever (see Heb 13:8).

Dear sons and daughters ... do not cease to proclaim that Jesus Christ is the only Savior; that His gospel can transform minds and hearts, bring about the desired reconciliation, and call ... all the earth's peoples to true brotherhood devoid of hatred or distrust. You must be Christians who are familiar with the revealed Word, with the Church's social and moral teaching, as well as with the demands of justice and peace; committed to the service of charity and to your people's advancement; diligent in bringing together all your brothers and sisters, with respect for their different ways of thinking.

If the Church does not proclaim the truth and show love, who will? This is our irreplaceable mission for the year 2000 and forever. [EC]

Certainly, not everyone is called to set out on mission…. It is not important *where* but *how*. We can be authentic apostles, in a most fruitful way, even at home, at work, in a hospital bed, in a convent cloister…. What counts is that the heart burn with that divine charity which alone is able to transform into light, fire, and new life—for the whole of the Mystical Body and to the ends of the earth—not only physical and moral sufferings, but also our daily fatigue. [WM]

Seeing the many people who, although loved by the Father, have not yet been reached by the Good News of salvation, Christians cannot fail to note in their hearts the urgency which shook the apostle Paul, causing him to cry out, "Woe to me if I do not preach the gospel!" (1 Cor 9:16, RSV). To a certain degree, in fact, each of us is personally responsible, before God, for those millions of people who are without faith.

The size of the task and the recognition of the inadequacy of one's energies may at times lead to discouragement, but we need not fear: We are not alone. The Lord Himself reassures us: "I am with you always; yes, until the end of time" (see Mt 28:20)....

Let it be consoling, then, particularly in times of doubt and difficulty, to keep in mind that however praiseworthy and indispensable human efforts, mission is always primarily the work of God, the work of the Holy Spirit, the Counselor.... [WM]

There is no authentic Christianity if there is no mission activity.... Jesus is a gift from God that must be brought to everyone. [YR]

Spare no energy in promoting sacred art. It is well known how the specific nature of sacred art is not to be found in being merely a decorative veneer applied to other realities that would otherwise remain insignificant. In that case art would be reduced to an aesthetic embellishment of a formless subject.

We are well aware that in God, beauty is not a derivative attribute, but rather coincides with His own reality, which is "glory," as the Scriptures state: "Thine, O Lord, is the greatness, and the power, and the glory, and the victory and the majesty" (1 Chr 29:11, RSV). When the Church calls on art to assist her mission, it is not only for aesthetic reasons, but to obey the very "logic" of revelation and the Incarnation. It is not a question of sweetening man's bitter path with invigorating images, but of offering him even now the possibility of having an experience of God, who contains within Himself all that is good, beautiful, and true. [PC]

The martyrs are the most authentic witnesses to the truth about existence. The martyrs know that they have found the truth about life in the encounter with Jesus Christ, and nothing and no one could ever take this certainty from them. Neither suffering nor violent death could ever lead them to abandon the truth which they have discovered in the encounter with Christ.

This is why to this day the witness of the martyrs continues to arouse such interest, to draw agreement, to win such a hearing, and to invite emulation. This is why their words inspire such confidence: From the moment they speak to us of what we perceive deep down as the truth we have sought for so long, the martyrs provide evidence of a love that has no need of lengthy arguments in order to convince. The martyrs stir in us a profound trust because they give voice to what we already feel and they declare what we would like to have the strength to express. {FR 32}

Today the witnesses speak out:
not only the first ones, the eyewitnesses, but also those
    who, from them, have learned the Easter message
and have borne testimony to Christ crucified and risen
from generation to generation.
Some have been witnesses even to the shedding of their
    blood
and, thanks to them, the Church has continued on her way,
also amid harsh persecutions and obstinate rejection.
On the strength of this unending testimony the Church has
    grown,
and is now spread throughout the world.
Today is the feast of all witnesses;
including those of our own century, who have proclaimed
    Christ
in the midst of the "great tribulation" (see Rv 7:14),
confessing His death and resurrection
in the concentration camps and the gulags,
under the threat of bombs and guns,
amid the terror unleashed by the blind hatred
which has tragically engulfed individuals and whole nations.
Today they come from the great tribulation
and sing the glory of Christ:
in Him, rising from the shadows of death,
life has been made manifest. [UO]

Spirit of holiness,
Who pours out Your gifts on all believers,
and especially on those called to be Christ's ministers,
help young people to discover the beauty of the divine
  call.
Teach them the true way of prayer,
which is nourished by the Word of God.
Help them to read the signs of the times,
so as to be faithful interpreters of Your gospel
and bearers of salvation. [PV]

Mary, Virgin who listened
and Virgin of the Word made flesh in your womb,
help us to be open to the Word of the Lord,
so that, having been welcomed and meditated upon,
it may grow in our hearts.
Help us to live like you the beatitudes of believers
and to dedicate ourselves with unceasing charity
to evangelizing all those who seek your Son.
Grant that we may serve every person,
becoming servants of the Word we have heard,
so that remaining faithful to it
we may find our happiness in living it. [PV]

8
JOIN A SMALL CHRISTIAN COMMUNITY

So then you are no longer strangers and sojourners, but you are fellow citizens with the saints and members of the household of God.

EPHESIANS 2:19, RSV

The call to communion ... the Vine and the branches ... communion, the mystery of the Church ... communion in the parish ... small church communities ... instruments of holiness ... transformation through lay groups ... bearing fruit ... communion and mission ... in service of the community

The human person has an inherent social dimension which calls a person from the innermost depths of self to *communion* with others and to the *giving* of self to others. [CL]

"I am the vine, you are the branches" (Jn 15:5, RSV) [is] an image that sheds light not only on the deep intimacy of the disciples with Jesus but on the necessity of a vital communion of the disciples with each other: All are branches of a single vine. [CL]

From the communion that Christians experience in Christ there immediately flows the communion which they experience with one another.... In this communion is the wonderful reflection of and participation in the mystery of the intimate life of love in God as Trinity, Father, Son, and Holy Spirit, as revealed by the Lord Jesus. For this *communion* Jesus prays: "That they may all be one; even as You, Father, are in Me, and I in You, that they also may be in Us, so that the world may believe that You have sent Me" (see Jn 17:21). *Such communion is the very mystery of the Church.* [CL]

It is essentially the parish which gives the Church concrete life, so that she may be open to all. Whatever its size, it is not merely an association. It must be a home where the members of the Body of Christ gather together, open to meeting God the Father, full of love, and the Savior His Son, incorporated into the Church by the Holy Spirit at the time of their baptism, and ready to accept their brothers and sisters with fraternal love, whatever their condition or origins.

The parish institution is meant to provide the Church's great services: prayer in common and the reading of God's Word; celebrations, especially that of the Eucharist; catechesis for children and the adult catechumenate, the ongoing formation of the faithful; communication designed to make the Christian message known; services of charity and solidarity; and the local work of movements. In brief, in the image of the sanctuary which is its visible sign, it is a building to be erected together, a body to bring to life and develop together, a community where God's gifts are received and where the baptized generously make their response of faith, hope, and love to the call of the gospel. [AL]

Internal to the parish,... *small Church communities* ... can be a notable help in the formation of Christians. They provide a consciousness and an experience of ecclesial communion and mission which are more extensive and incisive. [CL]

Whatever association of the lay faithful there might be, it is always called to be more of an instrument leading to holiness in the Church, through fostering and promoting a more intimate unity between the everyday life of its members and their faith. [CL]

C hurch communion, already present and at work in the activities of the individual, finds its specific expression in the lay faithful's working together in groups, that is, in activities done with others in the course of their responsible participation in the life and mission of the Church. In recent days the phenomenon of laypeople associating among themselves has taken on a character of particular variety and vitality.... Such work is ... the source and stimulus leading to the transformation of the surroundings and society. [CL]

Bearing fruit is an essential demand of life in Christ and life in the Church. The person who does not bear fruit does not remain in communion: "Every branch of Mine that bears no fruit, he [My Father] takes away" (Jn 15:2, RSV).

Communion with Jesus, which gives rise to the communion of Christians among themselves, is an indispensable condition for bearing fruit: "Apart from me you can do nothing" (Jn 15:5, RSV). And communion with others is the most magnificent fruit that the branches can give: In fact, it is the gift of Christ and His Spirit. [CL]

Communion and mission are profoundly connected with each other; they interpenetrate and mutually imply each other to the point that *communion represents both the source and the fruit of mission: Communion gives rise to mission and mission is accomplished in communion.* It is always one and the same Spirit who calls together and unifies the Church and sends her to preach the gospel. [CL]

ecause of each member's unique and irrepeatable character—that is, one's identity and actions as a person—each individual is placed at the service of the growth of the ecclesial community while, at the same time, singularly receiving and sharing in the common richness of all the Church. This is the "communion of saints" which we profess in the creed. *The good of all becomes the good of each one, and the good of each one becomes the good of all.* [CL]

9
KNOW YOUR FAITH

*Continue in what you have learned and have firmly believed,
knowing from whom you learned it and how from childhood
you have been acquainted with the sacred writings which are
able to instruct you for salvation through faith in Christ Jesus.
All scripture is inspired by God and profitable for teaching, for
reproof, for correction, and for training in righteousness, that the
man of God may be complete, equipped for every good work.*

2 TIMOTHY 3:14-17, RSV

Christ, the heart of our faith ... faith and reason ... know
Christ above all else ... guardians of the truth ... the treas-
ure of the Scriptures ... the Catechism, God's gift to the
Church ... freedom and faith ... the necessity of belief ...
listening to the Spirit in Scripture ... the Word in the liturgy ... the authority of the Magisterium ... God's Word
and vocations ... God's revelation in nature ... true ecumenism and the unity of faith

Today there shines forth ... upon the whole world the face of God: Jesus reveals Him to us as the Father who loves us.
All you who are seeking meaning in life,
all you whose hearts are burning
with the hope of salvation, freedom, and peace,
come to meet the Child born of Mary.
He is God, our Savior,
the only One worthy of this Name,
the one Lord.
He is born for us; come, let us adore Him! [CE]

In the mystery of the Trinity, the journey of faith has its origin and its final goal, when at last our eyes will contemplate the face of God forever. In celebrating the Incarnation, we fix our gaze upon the mystery of the Trinity. Jesus of Nazareth, who reveals the Father, has fulfilled the desire hidden in every human heart to know God. What creation preserved as a seal etched in it by the creative hand of God and what the ancient prophets had announced as a promise is disclosed in the revelation of Christ. [IM]

Faith and reason are like two wings on which the human spirit rises to the contemplation of truth; and God has placed in the human heart a desire to know the truth—in a word, to know Himself—so that, by knowing and loving God, men and women may also come to the fullness of truth about themselves. [FR]

In the Incarnation of the Son of God we see forged the enduring and definitive synthesis which the human mind of itself could not even have imagined: The Eternal enters time, the Whole lies hidden in the part, God takes on a human face. The truth communicated in Christ's revelation is therefore no longer confined to a particular place or culture, but is offered to every man and woman who would welcome it as the word which is the absolutely valid source of meaning for human life.

Now, in Christ, all have access to the Father, since by His death and resurrection Christ has bestowed the divine life which the first Adam had refused (see Rom 5:12-15). Through this revelation, men and women are offered the ultimate truth about their own life and about the goal of history.... Seen in any other terms, the mystery of personal existence remains an insoluble riddle. Where might the human being seek the answer to dramatic questions such as pain, the suffering of the innocent, and death, if not from the mystery of Christ's passion, death, and resurrection? [FR 12]

Know Jesus Christ! Be the first to know Him. Through constant reading and meditation, through prayer which is a constant dialogue between life and the Word of Jesus....

Know the gospel.... Know the gospel by seeking help from wise guides and witnesses to Christ. Ask for help to know and live that love which is the heart of the gospel....

By knowing the gospel, you will encounter Christ— and do not be afraid of what He may ask of you. Because Christ is also demanding, thank God! He is demanding.... Were He not demanding, there would be nothing to listen to, nothing to follow. [YR]

The Scriptures are dear to all of us. They are one of the greatest treasures we share. In the Sacred Scriptures and in the deeds of divine mercy which they narrate, God our Father, out of the abundance of His love, speaks to us as His children and lives among us. The Bible is holy because in its inspired and unalterable words the voice of the Holy Spirit lives and is heard among us, sounding again and again in the Church from age to age and from generation to generation. [WB]

In personal reading of the Bible, just as in catechesis, it is necessary always to listen to the Spirit who enlightens the meaning of the texts (see 2 Cor 3:6). It is He who makes the Word alive and present, helping to grasp its worth and its demands. "Holy Scripture must be read and interpreted according to the same Spirit by whom it was written" [DV 12].

We are the guardians and messengers of the Good News. In all its forms the apostolate consists first of all in transmitting and preaching the Word of salvation, and knowledge of the Word who is the Way, the Truth, and the Life. God's Word alone can truly illumine each individual's path, give full meaning to family life, to professional activities and to the thousand tasks of social life, and open the way to hope. The Word we acclaim in the liturgy and for which we glorify God is directly addressed to the faithful who are present.

The assembly gathered together must itself be constantly evangelized: Each believer always needs to let himself be challenged by Christ and to be converted by listening to the Word which makes great demands but at the same time is a priceless gift—for it is the proclamation of salvation, reconciliation, and the victory of life over death. The preparation of the people to accept the Word of life is a fundamental mission of evangelization for communities. "That ... which we have heard ... which we have looked upon and touched with our hands, concerning the word of life" (1 Jn 1:1, RSV) we must proclaim from generation to generation. [AL]

The Catechism is truly God's timely gift to the whole Church and to every Christian at the approach of the new millennium.... The Catechism presents in a clear and complete way the riches of the Church's sacramental doctrine, based on its genuine sources: Sacred Scripture and tradition as witnessed to by the fathers, doctors, and saints, and by the constant teaching of the Magisterium. [SE]

Freedom is not realized in decisions made against God. For how could it be the exercise of true freedom to refuse to be open to the very reality which enables our self-realization? Men and women can accomplish no more important act in their lives than the act of faith; it is here that freedom reaches the certainty of truth and chooses to live in that truth. [FR 13]

The fool thinks that he knows many things, but really he is incapable of fixing his gaze on the things that truly matter. Therefore, he can neither order his mind (see Prv 1:7) nor assume a correct attitude toward himself or toward the world around him. And so when he claims that God does not exist (Ps 14:1), he shows with absolute clarity just how deficient his knowledge is and just how far he is from the full truth of things, their origin and their destiny. [FR 18]

There are in the life of a human being many more truths which are simply believed than truths which are acquired by way of personal verification. Who, for instance, could assess critically the countless scientific findings upon which modern life is based? Who could personally examine the flow of information which comes day after day from all parts of the world and which is generally accepted as true? Who in the end could forge anew the paths of experience and thought which have yielded the treasures of human wisdom and religion? This means that the human being—the one who seeks truth—is also the one who lives by belief.

In believing, we trust ourselves to the knowledge acquired by other people. This suggests an important tension. On the one hand, the knowledge acquired through belief can seem an imperfect form of knowledge, to be perfected gradually through personal accumulation of evidence. On the other hand, belief is often humanly richer than mere evidence, because it involves an interpersonal relationship and brings into play not only a person's capacity to know, but also the deeper capacity to entrust oneself to others, to enter into a relationship with them which is intimate and enduring. [FR 31, 32]

"O Lord, our Lord, how glorious is your name over all the earth!" (Ps 8:1, NAB). The visible world is like a map pointing to heaven, the eternal dwelling of the living God. We learn to see the Creator by contemplating the beauty of His creatures. In this world the goodness, wisdom, and almighty power of God shine forth. And the human intellect, even after original sin—in what has not been darkened by error or passion—can discover the Artist's hand in the wonderful works which He has made. Reason can know God through the book of nature: a personal God who is infinitely good, wise, powerful, and eternal, who transcends the world and, at the same time, is present in the depths of His creatures.

Saint Paul writes: "Ever since the creation of the world, His invisible attributes of eternal power and divinity have been able to be understood and perceived in what He has made" (see Rom 1:20). Jesus teaches us to see the Father's hand in the beauty of the lilies of the field, the birds of the air, the starry night, fields ripe for the harvest, the faces of children, and the needs of the poor and humble. If you look at the world with a pure heart, you too will see the face of God (see Mt 5:8), because it reveals the mystery of the Father's provident love. [YD]

In fulfilling the plan of Redemption, God wanted to ask mankind's collaboration: Sacred Scripture narrates the history of salvation as a history of vocations, in which the Lord's initiative and the people's response have become intertwined. In fact, every vocation is born from the meeting of two freedoms: the divine and the human. Having been personally invited by the Word of God, the one called places himself or herself at His service. In this way there begins a journey, not without difficulties and trials, which leads to a growing intimacy with God and to an ever-greater openness to the demands of His will.

In every vocational call God reveals the deep meaning of the Word, which is a progressive revelation of His Person up until the manifestation of Christ, the ultimate meaning of life: "He who follows me will not walk in darkness, but will have the light of life" (Jn 8:12, RSV). Therefore, Christ, Word of the Father, is the model for understanding the vocation of every man and woman, for verifying their life journey and giving spiritual fruitfulness to their mission. [PV]

L istening to divine Revelation [the Scripture], silent meditation, contemplative prayer, and its translation into life experience constitute the soil in which an authentic vocational atmosphere can flower and develop.... Listening to the Word opens the heart of individuals to the Word of God and contributes to the building up of the community, whose members in this way discover their vocation from within and educate themselves for a generous response of faith and love. Only the believer who has become a disciple can savor "the goodness of the Word of God" (Heb 6:5, RSV) and respond to the invitation to a life of special evangelical commitment. [PV]

There are times and circumstances when it is necessary to make decisive choices for the whole of life. We are experiencing ... difficult times in which it is often hard to distinguish good from evil, true teachers from the false. Jesus warned us: "Take heed that you are not led astray; for many will come in my name, saying, 'I am he!' and 'The time is at hand!' Do not go after them" (Lk 21:8, RSV).

Pray and listen to His words. Let yourselves be guided by true pastors. Do not ever succumb to the world's flattery and facile illusions, which frequently become tragic disappointments.... There are no shortcuts to happiness and light. [YP]

The Magisterium, whose authority is exercised in the name of Jesus Christ, is an organ of service to the truth and is responsible for seeing that the truth does not cease to be faithfully handed on throughout human history. Today we must recognize a widespread misunderstanding of the meaning and role of the Church's Magisterium. This is at the root of the criticism and protests regarding its pronouncements.... One of the decisive aspects that lies at the base of the malaise and uneasiness in certain parts of the ecclesiastical world [is] a question of the way authority is conceived. In the case of the Magisterium, authority is not exercised only when the charism of infallibility is invoked; its exercise has a wider field, which is required by the appropriate defense of the revealed deposit.

For a community based essentially on shared adherence to the Word of God and on the resulting certainty of living in the truth, authority for determining the content to be believed and professed is something that cannot be renounced.... It therefore seems urgently necessary to recover the authentic concept of authority—not only from the formal juridical standpoint, but more profoundly, as a means of guaranteeing, safeguarding, and guiding the Christian community in fidelity to and continuity with tradition, to make it possible for believers to be in contact with the preaching of the apostles and with the source of Christian reality itself. [CD]

Theology can never be reduced to the private reflection of a theologian or a group of theologians. The Church is the theologian's vital environment, and in order to remain faithful to its identity, theology cannot fail to participate deeply in the fabric of the Church's life, doctrine, holiness, and prayer. This is the context in which the conviction that theology needs the living and clarifying word of the Magisterium becomes fully understandable and perfectly consistent with the logic of the Christian faith. [CD]

The commitment to ecumenism is of primary importance for the Christian. It is in fact known that Jesus prayed at the Last Supper for the unity of His disciples, with heartfelt intensity: "As You, Father, are in Me, and I in You, I pray that they may be [one] in Us, that the world may believe that You sent Me" (Jn 17:21, NAB).

Jesus did not hesitate to pray to the Father for His disciples "that their unity may be complete" (Jn 17:23, NAB) in spite of the difficulties and tensions He knew they would encounter. He Himself had noticed the disagreements between the twelve even during the Last Supper, and foresaw those which were shortly to appear in the life of the Christian communities, scattered throughout such a vast and varied world. Nonetheless, He prayed for the complete unity of His followers, and for this end He offered the sacrifice of His own life. [MC]

In view of the present divisions among Christians, there might be a temptation to think that the unity of Christ's Church does not exist or that it is merely a beautiful ideal to strive for but which will only be achieved in eschatology. However, the faith tells us that the Church's unity is not only a future hope: It already exists. Jesus Christ did not pray for it in vain. Nevertheless, unity has not yet reached its visible achievement among Christians and indeed, as is well known, down the centuries it has been subject to various difficulties and trials....

Thus the problem of ecumenism is not to bring about from nothing a unity that does not yet exist, but to live fully and faithfully, under the action of the Holy Spirit, that unity in which the Church was constituted by Christ. In this way the true meaning of prayer for unity and of the efforts made to further understanding among Christians becomes clear. Creating agreements is not merely a question of gathering together people of goodwill; rather, it is necessary to accept fully the unity desired by Christ and continuously bestowed by the Spirit. This cannot be reached simply by convergences agreed on from below. Rather it is necessary for each to be open to sincerely accepting the impulse that comes from on high, docilely following the action of the Spirit who wants to unite men in "one flock" under "one Shepherd" (see Jn 10:16), Christ the Lord. [DF]

The Good Shepherd desired that down the centuries His voice of truth should be heard by the whole flock He purchased by His sacrifice. This is why He entrusted to the eleven with Peter as head, and to their successors, the mission to watch like sentries so that the *una, sancta, catholica, et apostolica Ecclesia* [the one, holy, Catholic, and apostolic Church] might be realized in each of the particular Churches entrusted to them. Thus in the communion of pastors with the bishop of Rome there is achieved the witness to truth that is also a service to unity, in which the role of the successor of Peter has a very special place.

At the dawn of the new millennium, how can we not invoke for all Christians the grace of that unity merited for them by the Lord Jesus at so high a price? *The unity of faith*, in adherence to revealed Truth; *the unity of hope*, in the journey towards the fulfillment of God's kingdom; *the unity of charity*, with its multiple forms and applications in all areas of human life. In this unity all conflicts can be resolved, and all separated Christians can find reconciliation, in order to reach the goal of full and visible communion.

And should we ask if all this is possible, the answer will always be yes. It is the same answer which Mary of Nazareth heard: With God, nothing is impossible. [DF]

A Final Prayer for
the Jubilee and Beyond

L ord Jesus, Lord of history, who came at the fullness of time, prepare our hearts to celebrate with
faith the great Jubilee of the Year 2000, that it may
be a year of grace and mercy. Give us a heart that is
humble and simple, a heart that knows how to contemplate with an ever-increasing wonder the mystery of the
Incarnation, for You, Son of the Most High, You have
become our Brother in the womb of the Virgin Mary,
sanctuary of the Spirit.

Jesus, origin and fulfillment of the new man, turn our
hearts to You, that we may abandon the paths of error
and walk in Your footsteps, on the road that leads to life.
Enable us to live our faith fully according to the promises
we made at baptism. May we be, therefore, fearless witnesses of Your Word so that the life-giving light of the
gospel may shine forth in our families and in society.

Jesus, power and wisdom of God, create in us a love
for Holy Scripture where the voice of the Father
resounds, the voice that enlightens and inflames, that
nourishes and consoles.

Word of the Living God, renew the missionary thrust of the Church, so that all people may come to know You, true Son of God and true Son of Man, the one Mediator between man and God. Jesus, source of unity and peace, strengthen the bonds of unity within Your Church, intensify the ecumenical movement, so that Your disciples, through the power of Your Spirit, may all be one.

You who have given to us as a rule of life the new commandment of love, transform us into builders of a world truly united, where war gives way to peace and the culture of death to a commitment to life.

Jesus, only Son of the Father, full of grace and truth, Light which enlightens all men, give Your life in abundance to those who seek You with a sincere heart.

To You, Redeemer of mankind, the Beginning and the End of time and of the universe, to the Father, inexhaustible Source of all good, to the Holy Spirit, Seal of infinite love, all honor and all glory forever and ever! Amen. [JP]

ABBREVIATIONS

AL *Ad Limina* address to the bishops of France, January 25, 1997

AP Address to Cardinal William W. Baum and the Apostolic Penitentiary, March 22, 1996

AR Homily at a Mass at Aqueduct Racetrack in Queens, N.Y., October 6, 1995

BE Message on the Fourth U.N. Conference on Women, May 26, 1995

CC Homily at Sunday Mass, World Youth Day, Cherry Creek State Park, Denver, Colo., August 15, 1993

CD Address to the Congregation for the Doctrine of the Faith at the conclusion of their plenary session, November 24, 1995

CE Christmas Eve homily, Midnight Mass, December 24, 1997

CH Christmas Message to Children, December 13, 1994

CL *Christifidelis Laici,* December 30, 1988, nn. 18, 29, 30

CM *Urbi et orbi,* Christmas Message, December 25, 1994

CP Catechesis on prayer during a general audience, September 9, 1992

CU Address to the pontifical council "Cor Unum," April 18, 1997

DD *Dies Domini,* Pentecost Sunday, May 31, 1998

DF *"Di fronte alle,"* 137th address on the mystery of
the Church, August 30, 1995

DS Speech at Stapleton International Airport, Denver,
Colo., August 12, 1993

DV *Dominum et Vivicantem,* May 18, 1986, nn. 12,
65

EC *"En esta occasion,"* message to the Church in
Cuba, February 2, 1996

EH Address to a convention, "The Environment and
Health," March 24, 1997

EL Address at an ecumenical Liturgy of the Word
with representatives of non-Catholic churches in
Germany, June 22, 1996

EP Address at an ecumenical prayer service in Poland,
May 31, 1997

EV *Evangelium Vitae,* March 25, 1995, n. 83

FA Address at the 28th Conference of the U.N. Food
and Agriculture Organization, October 23, 1995

FC *Familiaris Consortio,* nn. 59, 60

FR *Fides et Ratio,* September 18, 1998, greeting, 12,
13, 16, 18, 27, 31, 32, 92

FS Address to the World Food Summit, November
13, 1996

GE Address to the World Congress of Gynecological
Endoscopy, June 21, 1997

GT "Give Them Something to Eat," Message for
Lent, 1996, September 8, 1995

HC Address at a conference sponsored by the
Pontifical Council for Pastoral Assistance to
Health-Care Workers, November 30, 1996

HE General audience on the Holy Eucharist in the life of the Church, April 8, 1992

HS Address on the United Nations Conference on Human Settlements, June 16, 1996

HW Catechesis on the dignity of human work, March 19, 1997

IM *Incarnationis Mysterium,* Bull of Indictment of the Great Jubilee of the Year 2000, November 29, 1998

JP Prayer for the First Year of the Immediate Preparation for the Great Jubilee Year 2000, January 14, 1997

LB Letter to the bishops of the United States on the recent scandal given by members of the clergy, June 11, 1993

LC Letter to President Clinton, released April 5, 1994, by the U.S. Embassy to the Vatican

LP "Learning to Pray," September 1, 1980

MC 132nd address on the mystery of the Church, July 12, 1995

MD Address for World Migration Day, July 25, 1995

MF Second World Meeting with Families, October 5, 1997, Rio de Janeiro

MS Message for World Mission Sunday, May 28, 1996

MW "Motherhood, Woman's Gift to Society," address to an international meeting promoting the well-being of women, December 7, 1996

NE *Ad limina* address to the bishops of New England, September 21, 1993

NY Homily at a Mass in New York's Central Park, October 7, 1995

OP Homily at a Mass at Oriole Park at Camden Yards, Baltimore, Maryland, October 8, 1995

OR *L'Osservatore Romano,* English edition.

PA Address to a joint session of all the Pontifical Academies, November 28, 1996

PC Address to the Pontifical Commission for the Cultural Heritage of the Church, October 12, 1995

PL Address to the Pontifical Academy for Life, November 20, 1995

PP Message to the world's leaders and all people of goodwill on a particular aspect of peace, December 8, 1992

PS Address to the First World Congress for pilgrimage leaders and directors of pilgrimage shrines, February 28, 1992

PV Message for the World Day of Prayer for Vocations, October 28, 1996

RP *Reconciliatio et Paenitentia,* (1984) n. 12

SE *Ad limina* address to the bishops of Alabama, Kentucky, Louisiana, Mississippi, and Tennessee, June 5, 1993

SL "The Season of Lent," Message for Lent 1997, October 25, 1996

SP General audience on the Sacrament of Penance, April 15, 1992

SS Address to the Pontifical Academy of Social Sciences, April 25, 1997

TC Address to associations belonging to the Italian Federation of Therapeutic Communities, June 26, 1995

UN Address to the U.N. General Assembly, October 5, 1995

UO *Urbi et orbi,* Easter Sunday, April 12, 1998

WB Address at Williams-Brice Stadium, Columbia, S.C., September 11, 1987

WC Message for the 31st World Communications Day, January 24, 1997

WD Address on the World Day of Peace, December 8, 1996

WM Message for World Mission Sunday, May 18, 1997

WP Message for the 25th World Day of Prayer for Peace, January 1, 1992

YD Address to the 8th World Youth Day, Denver, Colo., August 14, 1993

YP Message for the 11th World Youth Day in 1996, November 26, 1995

YR Address to the youth of Rome in Saint Peter's Square, March 20, 1997